FRIENDLY FIRE WHITEWASH

Friendly Fire Whitewash

How the Coventry Fusilier Lee Thompson was Killed in the Gulf War and Why the Government Covers up the Truth

DENIS MacSHANE

First published in Great Britain by:
Epic Books for the
Justice for Lee Thompson Gulf War Friendly Fire Victim Committee
PO Box 41, Coventry CV2 1TW

Epic Books is the publishing division of the European Policy Institute.
19 Acfold Road, London SW6 2AJ.

ISBN 1 874379 00 9

Printed by the Russell Press Ltd, Nottingham.
Distributed by Spokesman Books, Gamble Street, Nottingham.
Tel. 0602 708318

To the world he was a soldier.
To me he was the world

Epitaph on the grave of a British soldier killed in the desert in World War Two.

CONTENTS

Introduction

It was shortly after eight in the morning on a frosty February day in a small village in France under the Jura mountains which flank the north of Lake Geneva. I was helping my wife, Nathalie, give breakfast to our two small daughters while waiting to take the oldest, three-year-old Sarah, to her nursery school. Then it would be on to work in Geneva at the International Metalworkers' Federation, the international coordinating federation for all the car, engineering, steel, aerospace and electrical trade unions in the world.

By a strange coincidence a young woman from Coventry had married a Frenchman who worked just across the border in Switzerland but had chosen to live in the same village as us in France. Michaela came in regularly to help look after the children when Nathalie or I were away working.

The coincidence lay in the fact that I knew Coventry well and had spent some of the happiest years of my working life in the city. Working for the BBC in the West Midlands in the 1970s I had covered Coventry industrial and political affairs. I produced my first ever radio programme on the 30th anniversary of the bombing of Coventry during the war. I had reported on the birth-pangs of Warwick University when the radical historian E.P. Thompson, then a history professor at Warwick, had exposed the keeping of secret files on students by the university administration. I had gone regularly on Saturdays to report on the Sky-Blues, the Coventry City football team that the managerial and promotional (some said self-promotional) genius of Jimmy Hill had raised from the doldrums of the lower divisions to the heights of the Football League.

Committed to the Labour Party, I interviewed at length legendary Coventry politicians like Alderman George Hodgkinson or the city's two outstanding Labour MPs, Richard Crossman and Maurice Edelman. In 1974, aged 26, I stood for Labour as the parliamentary candidate in Solihull, next door to Coventry, and achieved the best Labour swing ever in this staunch Conservative seat. I was active as a trade unionist on the Executive Council of the West Midlands Regional TUC. Then the blow came. The BBC decided that I was too identified as a Labour Party activist in the West Midlands and that if I wanted to continue my BBC career I had to move to London. It was the start of an unhappy era in my life which only cleared up when I committed myself full-time to labour movement work, and in the 1980s to working for the cause of South African, Brazilian, Korean or Polish workers fighting against oppression and for political freedom and economic and social justice.

But I remained close to the West Midlands, visiting friends there, giving talks to labour movement meetings, and staying in touch with local politicians. I was delighted to be asked to be a guest lecturer at Warwick University in Coventry to talk about developments in the European and world trade union movement.

So Michaela, from Coventry and chatting in a way that I knew so well, was a connection to part of Britain that was part of me. But that morning as she pushed open the front door her eyes were puckered in tears.

"Sit down, pour yourself a cup of tea, what's the matter?" I said anxiously.

"It's Lee. He's been killed."

"Lee? Who's Lee?" I asked myself. Oh yes, there was a friend of Michaela's, a relative of some sort, who was fighting in the Gulf War. But it didn't make sense. Like everyone I had been riveted to the radio, television and newspapers since the start of the air attacks and then the land offensive which had begun at the beginning of the week. I had been repelled by the boasting triumphalism of some reporting and the glorification of high-tech death delivered as in a Nintendo game. As a former journalist, the censorship appalled me and I turned more to French television whose reporters had rejected the tight political control accepted by American and British television channels.

But one thing was clear in my head. The ground attacks were going incredibly well. The war was virtually over. The Iraqis had not fought and had hardly fired back. Scores of thousands of Iraqis had been killed or were dying, especially in the notorious "turkey shoot" as allied planes slaughtered those fleeing along the road to Basra from Kuwait City. But surely allied casualties were unbelievably light — almost entirely restricted to the poor devils who died in traffic accidents as the thousands of vehicles moved up and down the desert roads to supply the fighting army.

Yet here was Michaela sitting on a chair in the kitchen disconsolate. She had received a phone call the night before. Apparently, Lee Thompson, whose brother was married to Michaela's sister, had been killed in his Warrior armoured personnel carrier in the middle of the British advance into southern Iraq. And the worst of it was, said Michaela, he had been killed by his own side, by American aircraft.

In the weeks and months that followed she brought me in more bits of news and I followed the story in the English newspapers. Lee Thompson, a 19-year-old soldier serving in the 3rd Battalion of the Royal Regiment of Fusiliers, had been sitting in the back of his Warrior when it suddenly exploded. Quickly enough, it was learnt that US Air Force A-10 'Tankbuster' planes had been responsible.

But it was not until July that the official British Army report was published and this report refused to place the responsibility for the tragedy on anyone's shoulders.

Michaela, who together with her husband was back in Coventry for a holiday in the summer of 1991, came back to say that Mick and Barbara Thompson, Lee's parents, were convinced there was a Whitehall cover-up in order to avoid being critical of the Americans. This view was shared by other families and by those who survived the attack. Far from the memorial and other services helping to assuage the grief, the failure to tell the parents exactly what happened was making them more angry and more determined to get at the truth.

On a periodic visit to Coventry, I went round to call upon the Thompsons. They sat me down, gave me a cup of tea and with typical West Midlands hospitality, a large cob full of ham in case I was hungry, and told me their story. They showed me all the letters and documents and videos of interviews with survivors. They told me what Lee's comrades who had survived had said.

Clearly something did not add up. As I read the letters and reports it became apparent that far less than the available truth was being given to the Thompsons. After twenty years work, I had contacts in politics, in the legal world, in the defence business, in the United States and in Germany whom I could call upon to help. When a person suffers a violent death it is a fundamental human right that his or her family and the public should know the full details of how and why it happened.

It is an age-old right but still of great relevance in our time. In two countries which I know well — South Africa and Poland — where the struggle for democracy has involved great sacrifice, one of the most important legal-political fights has been for full inquests into a death when violence is involved and there are unclear aspects of the death.

To allow the authorities to bury the dead without telling fully all they know about how and why the death took place is to pass from a society of democratic accountability to one in which arbitrary rule is exercised.

Both Great Britain and the United States are democracies but there is an increasing desire, especially in Britain, to strengthen and centralise the secret control of the state over the activities of its citizens.

The campaign to get the full truth about how Lee Thompson and his eight comrades died is part of a process to transfer knowledge from the secret realm of the state to the open possession of its citizens.

Mick and Barbara Thompson did not and do not see it in those grand terms. Month after month they have been sending letters to the Prime Minister, John Major, or to the United States' President, George Bush. Each time, they feel that they have been brushed off. The interests of the state have been placed before the rights of the citizens.

I warned the Thompsons that to undertake any campaign could involve political and media pressure, accusations that they were stirring up what was best left forgotten, charges of political exploitation, or the view expressed to me by one prominent churchman in Coventry that they "should come to terms with their grief, not prolong it."

But truth is the best balm. To live in uncertainty about how your youngest son died — even if the proximate cause of death, the rocket attack by the US aircraft, is known — is to extend the grief. The best way to find peace of mind is to know what happened. This so far the Government has denied the Thompsons and the other families.

This short account is not a discussion of the rights or wrongs of the Gulf War. As far as Mick Thompson is concerned it was right for British troops to go to eject Saddam Hussein from his invasion and then murderously brutal occupation of Kuwait.

I have tried as far as possible to stick to what people have told me in England, Germany, and the United States, and the documented evidence such as parliamentary reports, letters and documents from the British and American governments, official accounts of the campaign and published books on the Gulf War and related subjects.

I am grateful to various friends including Katherine Livas, Jane Mills, Debbie Smith, Kay Manna, Don Stillman, Collin

Gonze, Mark Stephens, Bärbel Dohring, Gabrielle Krämer-Prein and Chris Jenkins who have read or edited parts of the manuscript or helped with information and logistics. I am deeply grateful to Marie-Rose Tudeau for her illustrations. Others I owe thanks to but they must remain anonymous.

Finally this account, which remains provisional, taking us up only to the first anniversary of the launch of allied attacks on Iraq, is dedicated to the memory of Lee Thompson and the eight soldiers-in-arms who died with him and to Mick and Barbara Thompson whose fight for the truth is in the best tradition of British decency and democratic values.

Denis MacShane
Coventry, January 1992

CHAPTER 1

The Red and White Hackle

It was 6.45 in the morning on Wednesday, 27 February 1991. In the Gulf, tanks of Britain's 1st Armoured Division were powering into Kuwait in the final phase of the 100-hour war. In Coventry, it was a dank West Midlands morning as the bell rang in a modest house close to the M6 skirting the north of the city.

As she hurried downstairs in her nightie and dressing gown to answer the doorbell ringing so early in the winter morning, Barbara Thompson saw through the frosted doorpane an unusual sight.

A red and white blur seemed to be bobbing about on the top of the caller's head. Before her hand could reach to open the door her heart collapsed as she knew what she was about to be told.

A kindly but tense looking man in army uniform addressed her in a soft Irish accent. "Good morning, Mrs Thompson, my name is Captain Sutton of the ..."

He did not have to continue. The red and white hackle adorning the caps and berets of the Royal Regiment of Fusiliers is one of the best-known identifications in the British Army.

There was an identical red and white hackle in a framed photograph over the mantelpiece. The last time Barbara Thompson had seen it being worn was when her 19-year-old son, Lee, had come home in his Fusiliers' uniform.

"As soon as I saw it, I knew what had happened," says Barbara Thompson. "We had been up until 4.30 or so in the morning watching the Gulf news on the television. I knew Lee wasn't going to come back, I just knew."

Upstairs, Barbara's husband, Mick, lay asleep. Only the week before Barbara had fetched him home from hospital after a heart attack.

"Is Mr Thompson in?" asked Captain Sutton. "I can tell him if you like."

"No, I'll tell him" she replied, but at that moment, the door burst open and in came Lee's older brother Paul, hastily dressed as he, too, realised what the early morning visit meant. "It's our Lee, isn't it, Mum?"

Behind him came the father, Mick Thompson, in pyjamas, to hear the official statement: "I'm very sorry to tell you but your son has been killed in action."

For Captain Sutton, an administrative officer in the Birmingham depot of the Territorial Army section of the Royal Regiment of Fusiliers, a soldier who had enlisted as a boy and who had been commissioned from the ranks, the bearing of such news was not uncommon.

Announcing casualties is no rarity for today's army. For more than 20 years, deaths in Ulster or the Falklands have provided work for the country's Captain Suttons. They must not call after 10 p.m. or before 7 a.m. but they must get to relatives before the news is announced officially on radio or television.

Al Sutton had been sitting at home on the night of 26 February also anxiously watching the television reports from the Gulf as his son was serving there as a medical orderly. When the phone rang, his wife turned white as she thought it was about her own son. It was the Army to say they needed a Fusiliers' officer to announce a KIA — Killed in Action — to the family of a dead Fusilier. They could not find the officer who was responsible for bearing such news in the Coventry area — Sutton's responsibility was Birmingham — but he readily agreed to go.

He didn't sleep that night, sitting up with his wife fitfully watching the television and trying to get right in his mind what to say and do. At 5 a.m. he dressed carefully in his uniform, got out an A-Z for the West Midlands and set off to find the small, well-hidden road, Foxfords Crescent, where the Thompsons live. He arrived early and sat in his car for thirty minutes composing his thoughts before getting out and ringing the front-door bell.

The Thompsons live in Alderman's Green, north of the city centre and unusually for that city of industrial migration, their grandparents were Coventry people. Mick and Barbara lived in the same street as children.

The West Midlands is looked down upon by snootier parts of England, particularly the South East, but anyone who comes from or who has lived there knows of family and neighbourly warmth rarely found in the snobbier parts of England. Mick Thompson is a life-long member of the Transport and General Workers Union, proud of his union card and able to draw upon wells of solidarity from family and friends during the days and months that followed.

Captain Sutton, who lives in neighbouring Solihull, was quickly adopted as a member of the family. He offered to telephone other relatives to tell them but Barbara and Mick waved the offer aside.

"Paul went across the road and told his sister and then Maggie, who worked with me at Walsgrave Hospital, came round to sit a bit," Barbara recalls.

Captain Sutton went off to come back a few hours later with a fax from the Army in his hands.

"They say Lee and eight other soldiers were killed by friendly fire from American A-10 aeroplanes. They were killed in the confusion of battle. I am terribly sorry."

Together they watched the 3.30 press conference given by General Schwarzkopf when the deaths were also announced.

In the front window of the Thompson's house hung a Union Jack. As the grief sunk in no one moved to take it down.

"Even when I knew the Yanks had killed him, I still supported our troops in the Gulf," said Mick Thompson. "The flag stayed there till they all came home."

That their son was not amongst them remains a loss hard to bear but pride of place amongst the Thompsons' Christmas cards in December 1991 was one from Lee's commanding officer with the simple message: "You are always amongst our thoughts."

Lee's elder brother had been a soldier and still lives in Germany after leaving the Army and marrying a German girl. The rest of the family still live in Coventry. Lee's brothers, Paul and Dean, have a small building business and work hard to make a go of it.

It is a close-knit family, solid, with their feet on the ground. The mutual support that each member was able to offer would be important in the months following Lee's death.

Mick Thompson has spent most of his working life in a bakery on the other side of the city. He has a droll sense of humour, gives the impression of a man who prefers to please and to get along, but beneath there is a toughness: he has always refused to be pushed around by unfair orders, whatever the job.

Not long after Lee left for the Gulf his father suffered a mild heart attack. The heart attack surprised Mick who at the age of 55 is trim in appearance and shows none of the outward signs of a heart attack victim. "I'm not a worrying person but inwardly you don't know. Lee going off to the Gulf was a tension for us all," he says.

Barbara Thompson is the organizer of the family. She has brought up her children to be neat and tidy and the house is impeccably kept. She is the one who has written all the letters to Prime Minister John Major, to the Coroner, and to President Bush. With the forensic skill of a Q.C. she has broken down the complexities of the issue and listed the key questions that have yet to be answered in the mystery of her son's death.

"I brought Mick back from the hospital on Valentine's day — a Thursday and then the following week Lee was killed," she recalls.

There was no pressure on Lee to join the Army. He had been good at sport at school but with unemployment rising in de-industrializing Coventry, the Army offered a job.

He was a popular boy who got on well with girls. Michaela Charlton, whose sister is married to Lee's brother Dean, was several years older than Lee who used to come round to sit with her. "I treated him like I treat my little brother but he talked to me in quite a different way."

In a letter sent from the Gulf, he teased his older brother, "Tell Paul I can still pull the girls even out here. Maybe one day I'll tell him the secret, well, it's an art really." He was obsessively neat and clean, showering twice a day and ironing his jeans and shirts himself. He was an achiever, setting himself targets and accomplishing them. At junior school he won the annual cross-country race three years in a row. At Caludon Castle Comprehensive School he played rugby and soccer and at the weekend turned out for local football teams.

While playing sport he suffered a knee injury that nearly ended his army career before it began. He tried hard for the Royal Marines but failed the entry test. Instead after initial training he had the choice of the Ordnance Corps, the Engineers, or the infantry.

His father had done national service in REME. "I told him to opt for that, it's a cushy number."

"No, Dad," Lee replied. "I want to see some action." His training with the Fusiliers was proceeding smoothly with Lee showing exceptional ability as a marksman when suddenly his knee gave way. For a time it seemed he would have to leave but Barbara Thompson wrote to the training depot's commanding officer asking for Lee to be given a chance to prove himself. On 1 February 1990 he took part in the passing out parade and, barely 18 years old, he joined the 3rd Battalion of the Royal Regiment of Fusiliers at their barracks in Hemer near Dortmund in north-west Germany.

He was assigned to 8 platoon in C Company — at the time the best company in the battalion so its surviving members still claim.

On New Year's Day, 1991, he arrived in the Gulf.

CHAPTER 2

"Oh God, I think it's going to be fun"

To begin there was no plan for the Fusiliers to take part in the action in the Gulf. Although the Fusiliers represent one of England's oldest infantry regiments with battle honours going back to the seventeenth century, the decisions as to which troops to send to a possible field of conflict are taken with little reference to history or tradition. The first British troops sent there — at a time when the official reason was given as protecting Saudi Arabia, the so-called Desert Shield operation — were from the 7th Armoured Brigade. The Desert Rats did not include the Fusiliers who were asked merely to stand by to provide some replacements.

By November 1990, Washington decided that war was necessary and President Bush ordered massive reinforcements to bring the US presence up to half a million men, the biggest single deployment since World War Two. London followed suit and ordered the entire 1st Armoured Division to the Gulf which meant the 4th Armoured Brigade, including the 3rd Battalion of the Royal Regiment of Fusiliers, were on their way.

Germany was stripped of more than half the British troops stationed there in order to reinforce the British presence in the Gulf. It was the biggest deployment of British forces in more than forty years.

At their base in Hemer in northern Germany, the Fusiliers worked hard to prepare for their mission. Vehicles were repainted in desert camouflage. Soldiers worked on their vehicles dressed in their cumbersome NBC (Nuclear-Biological-Chemical) warfare suits as the great fear at the time was that Saddam would launch chemical attacks on the allied troops.

Once in the Gulf, the training continued harder than ever. Full-scale battle exercises took place using live ammunition. Visits from dignitaries from London were politely tolerated. "There wasn't much to do," recalls one of Lee's friends who survived the attack on the Warriors. "They spent endless time working on vehicle recognition as we knew that we would be seeing all sorts of different vehicles and would have to decide quickly which were friendly and which were enemy." The Fusiliers were thoroughly tested on recognition of guns, vehicles, helicopters and aircraft. "If you failed a test, you were put through it again," recalled a member of 8 Platoon when I talked with him in Hemer months after the incident. The Fusiliers seemed to be taking the question of vehicle recognition as if their lives depended on it.

In the ten years prior to the invasion of Kuwait, Britain and other western countries had extended maximum political support to Saddam Hussein who was seen as a western bulwark against Iran's fundamentalist irredentism. The United States Assistant Secretary of State, John Kelly, told the Iraqi president in February 1990: "You are a force for moderation in the region and the United States wishes to broaden her relations with Iraq." It was more than political support. Western arms salesmen had been selling Hussein anything he wanted to buy so that, in addition to its easily distinguishable Soviet tanks and other vehicles, the Iraqi army was equipped with a considerable quantity of western equipment. A bewildering array of vehicles would confront each other when battle was finally joined.

Confirmation of the importance of vehicle recognition came at the end of January 1991 when the Iraqis launched a brief probe and captured the coastal town of Khafji in Saudi Arabia. In the fighting that took place a number of US marines were killed when their armoured personnel carrier was attacked by American aircraft. As an official British account of the Gulf War states:

> The problem of involuntary fratricide engagements caused the Coalition commanders considerable concern and, as a result of Khafji, a number of measures were introduced to prevent these tragic accidents. These included the displaying of brightly coloured panels and inverted Vs on Coalition vehicles together with the use of fire control lines.

Lee Thompson and other Fusiliers got to work painting the big black Vs on the sides and the top of their Warriors. One of the survivors of 8 Platoon described to me the size of the V on the top of the vehicles by holding his arms out at an angle, making a V about six feet across. In television film and photographs of the allied vehicles the Vs are clearly visible. To help identification from the air a bright fluorescent sheet — orange for commanders' vehicles and green for others — was tied down across the top of the Warriors behind the turret.

The Fusiliers worked hard to make sure the Vs were painted on in strong black paint and that the fluorescent sheets would not come off as a result of desert winds, storms or the hard pounding the vehicles might take as they moved into action. After the Khafji incident, their lives, they knew, might well depend on their work to make sure their Warriors could be easily identified.

Training continued into February as the air attacks on Iraq took their toll. To relieve the boredom of waiting the Fusiliers wrote letter after letter to their parents back in England. Every two or three days, the postman brought a "bluey" to the Thompsons in Coventry. A week before the land war started, Lee wrote back home:

"Hello Mum, Dad and Paul and how the devil are you all.

Just got your letter and I'm finding the weather at home very amusing. It's well into the summer out here. It's about 95 degrees and we're doing a bit of Battle preparation.

As you've probably heard on the news the ground forces are going in soon but I'm not saying much about it except expect me home in April some time.

The Iraqi division that we're going to fight is at 60 per cent fighting strength so you can see that after a couple more days' air attacks they should be softened enough to undertake our mission fairly easily. We all can't wait to get going and we're all ready. We're at 30 minutes' notice to move. The Iraqis are not going to know what hit them.

We expect to have our bit of the war done in 24 to 36 hours and then that's the war over for us. We just sit back and watch the Americans go after the Republican Guard.

There's no need to worry and we've been told that we don't expect to take many casualties. I'm looking forward to getting back and having my first pint of cold lager for a couple of months."

On Friday 22 February the commander of the 3rd Battalion was given his final orders confirming the Fusiliers' task of neutralizing a series of gun batteries inside Iraq. That evening President Bush gave a final ultimatum to Saddam Hussein — if by the evening of 23 February the Iraqis had not started withdrawing from Kuwait, the ground offensive would be unleashed. The Fusiliers clutched radios listening to the BBC World Service as does the whole world whenever a great crisis is taking place.

Lee Thompson sat down with his back against his Warrior, call sign 23, and wrote the last letter of his short life.

19/2/91

Well hello mum dad and paul and how the devil are you all. Just got your letter and im finding the weather at home very ammusing. Its well into the summer out here its about 95°c today and were doing a bit of Battle preperation.

As you've probably heard on the news that the ground forces are going in soon. but im not saying much about it except, expect me home in April some time.

The IRAQI division that were going to HAMMER, is at 60% fighting strength and weve been told that were not going in until there down to 56% so as you can see that after a couple more days of air attacks.

they should be softend enough to undertake our mission fairly easily. We all cant wait to get going and were all ready, weve got everything ready and were at 30 mins notice to move, The IRAQIS are not going to know whats hit them,

We expect to have our bit of the war done in 24 to 36 hours and then thats the war over for us. We just sit back and watch the american go after the Republican Guard force.

Theres no need to worry, and weve been told that we dont expect to take many casulties that us by the way. but the IRAQS are going to take THOUSANDS, our policy (3 section) is not to take prisoners. and if an iraqis looks in 2 minds wether to surrende or fight then we'll make up his mind for him and just shoot him its as easy as that, anyway its to much paperwork and hastle to take Prisoners of war

Im looking forward to getting back to having my first pint of cold lager for a caple of months. My money is mounting up in Germany and yesterday i put £100 (700 Riyals saudi money) into my post office account (national Savings)

Will you send I good photo of me because a girl in Rochdale who im writing to wants one, How is everybody at home and tell

"Dear Mum, Dad and Family,

Great News — we're going in. I hope they don't find a peaceful solution to it now. I'm so excited.

So I hope you don't mind but this might be my last letter for a bit.

I will be actually doing the job that I'm getting paid for and isn't it great.

I hope everyone at home is OK, and I might be home in a couple of weeks but that's only if they don't put up too much opposition which hopefully they won't. Do you know that I'm in the BIGGEST military operation in History. It's much bigger than D Day.

Old Saddam Hussein is going to get his arse well and truly kicked courtesy of 3 RRF.

I can't wait. All the aggression that all the lads have been storing up since we got out here is going to be unleashed and I don't fancy being on the end of it all. All the lads have written on their hand grenades 'With love from 3 Section 8 Platoon 3 RRF' just to let them know who's going to give it to them.

Oh God, I think it's going to be fun.

Say hello to the family for me please and get the beer in the fridge. I must go now, I'm going to sharpen my bayonet.

See you all soon,

Love,

Lee XXX."

On the evening of Sunday 24 February, the Fusiliers crossed the Iraqi border. Photographs of their vehicles and those of their American guides have been published and the most striking aspect is the giant black Vs thickly painted on doors of American jeeps or on the sides of the tracked Warriors.

The line of advance had been carefully planned beforehand. The Fusiliers would move north across the border into Iraq and then turn right to head east toward Kuwait. The Warriors advanced in twos and threes, each giving cover to other vehicles in the four-vehicle platoon. As needed, the Fusiliers would dismount to clear trenches or attack as infantrymen. For Lee Thompson it was a bumpy ride with his mates in the cramped space and stale air of the Warrior. The 9-person section consists of a driver, the commander and gunner in the turret, and six soldiers sitting three on each side, knee to knee, on narrow benches in the back compartment of the Warrior.

Quickly it became evident that the Iraqis were not putting up much of a fight. The advance was slowed down as hundreds, then thousands of Iraqi prisoners clogged up the area. The British troops had been set various objectives — mainly gun emplacements — to clear, but none of the Fusiliers carried out an infantry attack for which they had been trained. There was one incident in which an Iraqi soldier who had surrended suddenly started firing his AK47 and was shot dead by a Fusilier. This was the only officially recorded incident in which an Iraqi was shot dead by the British SA80 infantry weapon — today's equivalent of the infantryman's rifle. Despite all their preparation, Lee and his comrades were not to shoot their personal weapons in anger.

Each Iraqi emplacement had been given a code name chosen by the paratrooper commanding the 1st Armoured Division, Major General Rupert Smith. For some reason he had selected various metals as the code names and slowly the troops advanced first on Bronze, and then on Copper.

The weather was awful with high winds and sand storms making night sights useless. On the night of 25-26 February, the Fusiliers used their satellite navigation equipment to position themselves in the desert. The night was miserable and dawn was little better. The Fusiliers were unable to get any sleep, munching on chocolate bars and chatting to each other huddled in the back of their Warriors.

All morning, rain and then winds, which whipped up great clouds of dust, obscured the area. It was not until 2 p.m. on Tuesday 26 February that the Fusiliers were ready to attack their next objective, code-named Brass. By then the rain had stopped and the wind had dropped to provide a clear, sunny afternoon for desert warfare. A rocket salvo preceded the attack. "The noise was fantastic and even in the Warriors one could feel the ground trembling with the concussions of the explosions," writes the official historian of the battle.

C Company moved up firing at the gun emplacements and protecting the Sappers from the Royal Engineers who moved in to disable the Iraqi guns permanently. The battle was being fought exactly according to plan. The speed and force of the attacks persuaded any Iraqis that still had some fight left in them after the air and artillery attacks that discretion was definitely the better part of valour.

So far, for Lee and the other Fusiliers, the battle had been little different from the training exercises they had been going through so strenuously both in Germany and since they had arrived in Saudi Arabia. Resistance had been extremely light and by 2.30 in the afternoon on the second full day of the war they had yet to come under serious enemy fire.

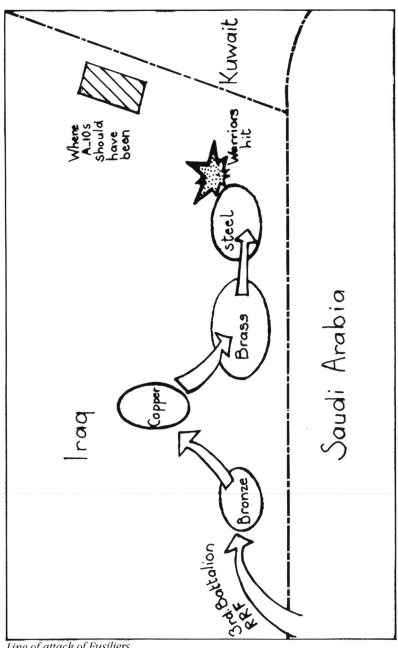

Line of attack of Fusiliers

CHAPTER 3

Death in the Afternoon

The fight to secure the Iraqi armour in the area code-named Brass was quickly over. C Company moved forward, now engaged in the successful momentum of a victorious drive to capture the gun emplacements in the objective code-named Steel. More than eighty vehicles carrying the 800 men in the 3rd Battalion were now moving forward over an area about a mile wide. The Warriors fight with their small 30 mm cannon, looking like a heavy machine gun sticking forward from the control turret. The gun is thin and short like a pea-shooter not quite reaching over the edge of the front of the armoured personnel carrier. It is utterly different from the long, heavy cannon of a battle-tank. The difference between a Warrior and a Soviet-made T 54/55 tank is the difference between say a Renault Espace and a big Mercedes. There is a difference in profile, in outline, in shape, and in tracks.

So far the Warriors had been used mainly as battle transport wagons with their canon and machine guns fired from the turret doing the main shooting. The six Fusiliers sitting in the back had had little chance to jump out through the back doors — 'dismount' is the elegant, cavalry redolent phrase the Army prefers — and go to work as foot soldiers.

At the front of the Battalion's advance were the 37 Fusilier and Engineer vehicles of C Company, which fancied itself as the best company in the battalion. And at the front of C company was 8 platoon. Its commander was 26-year-old Lieutenant Brett Duxbury who after seven years in the ranks had been commissioned in the Army Air Corps and was on loan to the Fusiliers as a platoon commander.

A few minutes before 3 p.m. on 26 February, the entire position was secured. "It was a straight-run to this objective. We didn't find any Iraqis there. Until then they had been all over the place trying to surrender," Duxbury later told Chris Jenkins, the *Daily Mail*'s Defence Correspondent. Jenkins, himself a former British Army captain and tank commander, fluent in German and French, and one of the world's experts on armoured vehicles, was able to interview Duxbury for an on-the-record account of the incident which was published in the *Daily Mail* when Duxbury's mention in despatches for bravery was officially gazetted.

The four Warriors in 8 Platoon had taken up position in a kind of elongated semi-circle around the Iraqi gun emplacement. The Warriors had charged up firing at the six Russian-made guns which were protected with sandbags but there were no Iraqi soldiers to fight back. The Fusiliers got out for a few moments' rest waiting for the Royal Engineers to arrive to blow up the weapons. The vehicles were about 50 yards away from the guns with men out smoking or having a pee in the sand.

When the Sappers announced they were ready to blow the guns, Duxbury ordered everyone back into the vehicles, and told them to batten down as a precaution against shrapnel from the explosion hurting anyone. The time was 3.02 p.m. The driver of one Warrior, Callsign 22, desperate for a smoke, disobeyed the order, leaving his driver's hatch half open to keep puffing. His disobedience probably saved his life because as he was taking a last long drag on his cigarette there was an immense explosion and he was propelled out of his Warrior.

"I thought it was a mine," the Fusilier recalls while Lieutenant Duxbury's first reaction was that "we were coming under artillery fire."

Duxbury and the platoon sergeant raced across the desert to help those in the burning Warrior. Four men died and others were wounded as the explosive-, shell-, and grenade-laden vehicle exploded. Those few minutes are forever etched in Duxbury's memory.

> There were bodies and wounded lying around who had to be attended to. The first task was to get more medical assistance. I ordered Callsign 23 on the far right to move in. As it moved there was another tremendous explosion. I saw five of the crew get out, including the commander and the driver.

Five other Fusiliers were killed, including Lee Thompson.

A kilometre away, the Commanding Officer, Lt. Col. Andrew Larpent could see the column of smoke above the two burning Warriors. He ordered up all help as quickly as possible, still concerned that it might involve an Iraqi attack. But he refused permission to ITN cameraman Nigel Thompson, an award-winning youthful veteran of conflict newsgathering, to go up to the scene. Larpent decided it was a sight not to be filmed. The Battalion's commander didn't refer up for guidance, he just decided that with the dead and wounded it was a scene which should stay private to the Army and he ordered the camera team to stay put. It was to be 24 hours before Thompson and ITN reporter, Paul Davies, were allowed to report on the tragedy and interview eye-witnesses.

The question of what people saw remains an issue of controversy. Duxbury thought it was artillery that had caused the explosion, while the driver of Callsign 22 believed it was a mine. Later when the parents met with members of 8 Platoon and C Company they heard Fusiliers talk of a lone aircraft in the sky, that swooped down very low before firing one rocket and then turning back to fire a second one. As it left the scene, it waggled its wings in the traditional pilot's V for Victory sign.

Another report talked of Fusilier radio operators swiftly tuning into the pilots' frequency and hearing that quickly the pilots had realised it was an error. One of them, so the story went, had broken down in his cockpit and his wingman had to talk him gently down to make a safe landing.

Certainly these memories (and the Fusiliers who believe they saw an A-10 come in low over the heads have provided independent witness statements) are in conflict with the official version such as it had been released to the parents. At the same time, BBC and other reporters who have interviewed survivors of the attack and other soldiers who were present do not report any person seeing or hearing an aeroplane prior to the explosions. Nigel Thompson, the ITN cameraman, whose eyes and ears are highly trained to pick up unusual sights and sounds as he trains his camera on the best image available neither heard nor saw an aeroplane. The driver of Callsign 22 had his hatch open a few inches in order to puff out his smoke when the Maverick rocket blasted into his Warrior. He, too, reports no memory of hearing or seeing a low-flying aircraft. Lieutenant Duxbury, an experienced soldier training to be a pilot, thought it had been artillery. For at least ten to fifteen minutes the Warriors had been still. The day was bright, clear, a desert afternoon when visibility is perfect and sounds carry far.

In the official reports, which will be examined in a moment, all references are to two A-10s, neither of which descended below 8,000 feet, according to the pilots' carefully prepared and dovetailed accounts. As we shall see, there are other major discrepancies in their accounts. Some of the soldiers on the ground say they saw a plane flying low, one even reports a third

The A-10 missiles kill nine soldiers

A-10 on the scene. Others are not so sure. The difference in memory is not the main issue which is simply why did the A-10s, whether at 8,000 or 500 feet, shoot their missiles at the clearly identified British vehicles?

None of these thoughts were in the minds of 8 Platoon and C Company as they raced to help their mates. Lt. Duxbury himself suffered a burst ear drum and had shrapnel in the side of his face. The platoon sergeant, Trevor Smith, was temporarily blinded by burns with serious shrapnel injuries in his legs. They spurned assistance as they tried to help save people from the burning Warriors.

The Warriors were packed with ammunition of all sorts — phosphorus grenades, anti-tank missiles and other explosive mixtures. Once hit and on fire they were lethal death-traps. Fusilier Simon Bakkor jumped on one burning Warrior to try and pull out the gunner trapped in the turret. It was in vain. An explosion blew Bakker off the turret embedding bits of armour plate in his thigh.

These were minutes of quiet heroism as men risked their own lives to save their comrades, unsure if another explosion — mine or artillery — would not bring further death and chaos. Soon more senior officers arrived and medical help. The wounded were given morphine injections and quickly evacuated. The dead bodies were retrieved from the vehicles.

For the Fusiliers the battle continued. Their next objective was code-named Tungsten, again an Iraqi defensive position manned by artillery and infantry. Salvoes or artillery and rocket fire from the British troops broke what was left of the morale of the Iraqi troops who surrendered en masse. The commander of Iraq's 27th Infantry Division emerged from his desert bunker "looking in pristine condition as if he had just been shopping in Harrods, in complete contrast to the ragged condition of his soldiers," notes the regimental account of the battle. The anonymous author goes on to state laconically: "His arrogance was somewhat dented when he learned that the Americans were now on the outskirts of Basra. He had further lessons in humility when dealt with by the Regimental Sergeant Major who was in charge of all prisoner handling."

By 4 a.m. on Wednesday 27 February, the Fusiliers had stopped fighting. After two sleepless nights, the soldiers grabbed a little rest. They had reached the border of Kuwait, the liberation of which was the principal objective of the war. The weather now changed to rainy grey skies. Late in the morning the Regiment's Padre conducted a short service for those who had been killed the previous day.

But by now the news was seeping out. The Fusiliers who died had not been killed by Iraqi mines or enemy artillery. They had been killed in action but killed by their own side, by American aircraft. The news shattered the Fusiliers, hitting C Company and the remaining 15 men in 8 Platoon worst of all.

Corporal Philip Forsyth told ITN the next day: "It was a total waste. Things were going so well. If we had jumped into the trenches and met the enemy face-to-face, round-to-round, bayonet-to-bayonet that would have been one thing but to be sitting in the back of the wagon and to be hit by friendly aircraft is unacceptable."

On 7 March, the Battalion band played as the coffins of the nine dead soldiers were loaded onto a transport plane for repatriation. At Brize Norton, another band and detachment of Fusiliers were present to honour the dead as they arrived. Most of the men who were killed — six Fusiliers and three members of the Queens Own Highlanders — were teenagers.

— Paul Atkinson from Tynemouth was 19
— Conrad Cole from Rochdale was only 17
— Neil Donald from Nairn in Inverness was 18
— Martin Ferguson from Inverness was 21
— Richard Gillespie from Tynemouth was 19
— John Lang from Edinburgh was 19
— Kevin Leech from Prudhoe, Northumberland celebrated his twentieth birthday on 23 February 1991, the day before the land war started
— Stephen Satchell from Rye was 18
— Lee Thompson from Coventry was born 9 September 1971 and was killed on 26 February 1991.

Their bodies were handed over to the families for funeral. At services held up and down the country the dead were buried. The struggle of the living to come to terms with their grief was just about to begin.

CHAPTER 4

High in the sky

For two pilots of the US Air Force, the early afternoon of Tuesday 26 February, 1991, was one of the most frustrating times of their lives. We do not know the names of the two pilots, nor those of any of the other pilots or controllers in the air or on the ground with whom they talked in the three hours and two minutes between take-off and unleashing the missiles that killed Lee Thompson and his comrades. They flew the A-10 "Tankbuster" plane, an ugly, low-speed jet, armed with cannon, machines-guns, and 48 deadly Maverick missiles, one of the most effective air-to-ground missiles yet developed. Designed for close ground support of troops facing armour the A-10s are sluggish donkeys of the sky that pack a most lethal punch. They had performed sterling work in attacking Iraqi armour during the air offensive. In Europe, they had practised flying very low so that ground controllers could direct them to the most useful targets in a battle exercise. But the A-10s' choice of tactics was what was known as "theatre-specific" and in the desert they had generally flown steadily at an altitude of more than 6,000 feet, safe from most small arms fire from the ground.

That morning the pilots had a lengthy briefing at their base. They "received an intelligence briefing on the situation" including "an as accurate as possible description of friendly and enemy troop positions." By then the troops were racing forward so rapidly that no positions were stable but, in general, they were advancing exactly according to the plans laid down by the allied general staff, so the pilots, in theory, should have been aware of where friendly troops were and what the line of advance was to be.

At noon they took off. "The weather en route was very poor and we were in clouds for the 45 minutes to the tanker." They almost missed their refuelling rendezvous and one A-10 was down to zero fuel before he found a tanker to pump fuel into his plane. At this stage they contacted an airborne Controller in one of the giant AWACS Boeings equipped with radar that

FRIENDLY CASUALTY REPORT

TO: USCENTCOM CMDR J3-OA
     ATTN: MAJ MASON ext 6231

     9 July 91

At approximately 1430L on 26 Feb 91, I, the flight lead of ████
██, a two-ship of A-10's, was handed off from ██████ on Tad
121 to ████ on Tad 07 for retasking. ██████ had us change to
Tad 53 to go active for the tasking. We were passed to
████████ and he directed us to proceed to ████ and to contact
████████ on Tad 209, and he advised me that there might be a ___ ___
████████ working the area. I made contact with ██████ on Tad
209 and he told me to continue towards the contact point of ██
Within seconds of my acknowledgement of ████████'s instructions,
██████, came up on frequency and said that he was departing the
area Bingo for fuel, but wanted to pass us information about the
area first.

I visually sighted what appeared to be a single F-16 to the SW of
██, and ████████ continued to pass target area information. He
described a North/South and East/West hardball intersection to
the East of ███████████████████████████ He said
there was a ██████ at the intersection and it was
unmistakable. "Going East from there on an approximate heading
of ██ will be another intersection of dirtball roads, one going
due East. East of that intersection three to four miles are two
burning hulks that we just attacked." He said there were more
vehicles in the area, in revetments as well as movers. When I
asked him about threats in the area, he said he had not observed
any. He then left the area - those were his last words to us.

We road recce'd the area, identified the ████████████ and the
hardball road intersection, and proceeded easterly on a ████
heading. ████████ came up and said simply "There are no
friendlies within 10 kliks." I saw two burning hulks trailing
black smoke to the west, and two more hulks along an Easterly
running dirtball road. Everything was fitting ████████
description of the target area that ████████ didn't add to. I
found a truck in a "bulldozer" style revetment and used my
binoculars to have a look at it. It looked like a supply
vehicle, so we strafed it. There was no threat observed in the
area, and that fit with ████████'s experience. I came off my
last strafe pass generally southbound, and it was then, about one
mile south of the supply truck we strafed, that I saw about 50
vehicles on the move northbound. I had ████ go cover for two
binocular passes-one at 15000 feet and another at 9000 feet. No
friendly markings ████████████████████████████████
██████ were observed. By all appearances, I thought they were T-
54/55 tanks and associated support vehicles. They were well
inside the 10 kilometer circle that ████████ had passed that no

2

friendlies would be in. We went south for standoff while I was climbing back to altitude, and I had marked the vehicles position as I overflew them with my INS. I launched one IR Maverick from station 9 at approximately 1502L. I came off and gained energy to cover for ▮▮▮ who launched his IR Maverick at approximately 1506L. I shot at the furthest north vehicle, and ▮▮▮ shot at the one to it's west. ▮▮▮▮▮ came up and asked me repeatedly what coordinates we were working at, and as I had marked the vehicles position...I toggled up the INS and read him ▮▮▮▮▮. The full 8 digit was ▮▮▮▮▮ I recovered the flight into ▮▮▮ after passing BDA to ▮▮▮▮▮ on Tad 15.

I wish to reiterate and make clear certain items.

1. No target coordinates were ever passed to me from either ▮▮▮▮ or from ▮▮▮▮▮ I derived the coordinates of the area I attacked by a direct overflight and marking on the INS. Those are the coordinates I passed to ▮▮▮▮ This may not have been clear on my prior message.

2. ▮▮▮▮ had said, following ▮▮▮▮▮ s target area description, that there were no friendlies within 10 K's. The center point of the 10 k's was understood to be the burning hulks that ▮▮▮▮ had described to me. The coordinates that I hit were within the 10 K circle by a wide margin.

3. Two binocular passes were made and even with the naked eye, friendly ▮▮▮▮ could be observed on other vehicles during the war at 15000 feet. No friendly ▮▮▮▮ were observed on any of the vehicles I searched, and using binoculars at 8000 feet gave me a clear picture. The weather in the area was clear.

4. I have **NEVER** heard the word ▮▮▮▮ in reference to this war except in this message traffic. Never was it transmitted to me during the entire course of the war.

I hope this answers any questions you may have.

directed the air attacks. The two A-10s were "tasked" or "directed to a contact point" over part of the battlefield. They flew on keeping an eye on the fuel. Visibility had now improved with cloud cover beginning at 17,000 to 18,000 feet but when they arrived at the area they were meant to attack, they found "the ground had become obscured by blowing sand."

They were "unable to work that target", to use the US Air Force jargon, so they contacted again the airborne controller in the AWACS, to ask for guidance and a target to attack. With his hands full, the airborne controller quickly gave them another contact point to aim for and told them to contact the Air Support Operations Centre (ASOC). It was now 2.30 in the afternoon. The A-10s had been in the air for more than two hours, flying around aimlessly unable to find anything to shoot at. They set off for their new destination, hoping that finally they could take part in the war.

With some difficulty they contacted the ASOC who then passed them on to the forward air controller, a British officer whose duty it was to guide all air attacks in the area being fought over by the 1st Armoured Division. But at the same time, the A-10 pilots established contact with one of their own comrades, the pilot of an F-16 fighter. He described to them an Iraqi target. If the planes turned East, towards Kuwait, they would come to a crossroads where a North-South road met a West-East road. If they then followed the road East, they would find some juicy targets — some Iraqi vehicles, two of which were burning after the fighter plane attacks. As he was taking in this information the lead A-10 pilot saw out of the corner of his eye "what appeared to be a single F-16" leaving the scene to his left and behind the A-10s. He assumed that this was the F-16 with which he had been talking.

At long last, the A-10s felt they had something to shoot at. They found a road, and then a crossroads which appeared to fit the description given to them by the F-16 pilot. But as the detailed maps of the area show there are many low-grade straight roads intersecting in the desert. The A-10s turned to follow the road east. The A-10 pilots saw the burning hulks and then saw more lorries. Despite all the high technology, laser, videos, computerized navigation system with which the US Air Force fought the Gulf War, the role of the human eye still played a key part. Each A-10 pilot is equipped with high-powered binoculars in order to carry out a final visual check before attacking any target. This requirement of course is suspended when the enemy is firing back but in the Gulf land war, the supporting aircraft did not face any threat from the ground.

The A-10 pilot got out his binoculars and identified what he considered to be Iraqi supply vehicles. He felt confident about what he was attacking because by now he made contact with the British controller on the ground who assured that there would be no "friendlies within a ten kilometer radius" of his position.

Saving his Maverick missiles for better-armoured targets, he launched his plane on an attack dive. As the Iraqi lorries came into his sights, he pressed the button to fire his machine gun. To his dismay he saw that he had missed. All the training, all the hours watching Errol Flyn or John Wayne in World War Two movies shooting up the Japs or Nazis with their bam-bam-bam machine guns, and here he had a sitting target and he had failed completely to hit it.

There could not be another miss. The next time he would unleash a Maverick missile. That was just a question of pushing a button and the missile would do the rest of the work.

So far, this account has been based on the reports submitted by the two A-10 pilots in July 1991, after the British had asked the Americans for their version of what happened. Copies of the reports, with a great deal of key information blacked out, were released to the parents by the US administration in November.

From now on, the pilots' account is flatly contradicted by all other evidence and by common sense. Let us stay with what the pilots said happened but remember that their account was written months after the incident and at a time when they knew that a major storm was breaking over the tragedy they had caused.

Having failed in their attempt to strafe the Iraqi trucks, the pilots flew on south and then saw another target, "about 50 vehicles on the move northbound." While the second A-10 circled, the lead pilot examined the target, first at 15,000 feet and then, again with his binoculars, at 8,000 feet. For people in Britain, 8,000 feet seems very high, nearly twice the height of Snowdon or Ben Nevis. But people who go skiing regularly ski at 8,000 feet and higher. In the 1992 winter Olympics in France, people in chairlifts or cable cars swayed at 8,000 feet and saw quite clearly what was going on on the ground below. With the help of binoculars, small details can be picked up on cars or lorries.

The A-10 pilot declared afterwards in his report that in his experience "even with the naked eye," friendly markings "could be observed on vehicles at 15,000 feet" twice as high as he now was flying. And yet he insists in his report that after two passes over the target, one at 15,000 feet and one at 8,000 feet, in which he used his binoculars, he could see none of the inverted Vs, nor the bright fluorescent panels. The fatal moment was now at hand.

> Instead of the British Warriors, the A-10 pilot said by all appearances, I thought (the vehicles) were T54-55 tanks and associated support vehicles. They were well inside the 10 kilometer circle that ▇▇▇▇▇▇ (presumably the British ground controller, DALO,) had passed that no friendlies would be in. We went south for standoff while I was climbing back to altitude, and I had marked the vehicles position with my INS (Inertial Navigation System). I launched one Maverick at approximately 1502. I came off and gained energy to cover for ▇▇▇▇▇▇ (presumably the name of the second A-10 pilot) who launched his Maverick at approximately 1506. I shot at the furthest north vehicle and ▇▇▇▇▇ shot at the one to it's (sic) west. ▇▇▇▇▇▇ (presumably DALO) came up and asked me repeatedly what coordinates we were working at, and as I had marked the vehicles position I toggled up the INS and read him ▇▇▇▇▇▇ (unclear). The full 8 digit was ▇▇▇▇▇▇ (presumably the grid reference).
>
> I wish to reiterate and make clear certain items.
>
> 1. No target coordinates were ever passed to me from either ▇▇▇▇▇▇ (presumably ASOC, the US Air Support Operations Centre) or from ▇▇▇▇▇ (presumably DALO). I derived the coordinates of the area I attacked by a direct overflight and marking on the INS. Those are the coordinates I passed to ▇▇▇▇▇▇ (presumably DALO).
>
> 2. ▇▇▇▇▇▇ (presumably DALO) had said, following ▇▇▇▇▇▇'s (presumably the F-16) description, that there were no friendlies within 10 K's. The center point of the 10 k's was understood to be the burning hulks that ▇▇▇▇▇▇ (presumably the F-16) had described to me. The coordinates that I hit were within the 10 K circles by a wide margin.
>
> 3. *Two* binocular passes were made and even with the naked eye, friendly ▇▇▇▇▇▇ (presumably markings) would be observed on other vehicles during the war at 15,000 feet. *No* friendly ▇▇▇▇▇▇ (presumably markings) were observed on any of the vehicles I searched, using binoculars at 8,000 feet gave me a clear picture. The weather in the area was clear.

So according to this account, the A-10 pilots had attacked Iraqi T54/55 tanks that were proceeding in a northerly direction, roughly in parallel with the Iraqi-Kuwaiti border. They had selected the targets themselves after getting information from

Warrior

T 54/55

Spot the difference

the departing F-16 plane and then getting the go-ahead from the British forward air controller to shoot at anything in a 10 kilometer radius. They accomplished their mission successfully and flew to refuel from a tanker and then head home.

Like most of the Hollywood films that have delighted us in recent years from the *Gremlins* to *Terminator 2*, from *The Empire Strikes Back* to *The Raiders of the Lost Ark*, the account of the American pilots was pure fantasy.

What was all too real were the nine dead and eleven wounded they had left on the ground as they flew away, target destroyed, mission accomplished, the frustrations of the first hours dissolved in the short-lasting knowledge that they had shot off their rockets in combat conditions.

CHAPTER 5

"We deeply regret ..."

As soon as the news of Lee's death came, the letters started arriving. The Army looks after the memory of its dead. It is a task each officer dreads — the writing of a letter to the family of someone who died under his command. The words do not differ much yet there can be no standardized letter. Each officer must get out paper, pen and ink, sit down, clear his mind, and wait for the right words to come.

Honouring and paying tribute to the dead has three functions for the military. Firstly, it justifies the business they are in, that of training themselves to be efficient killing machines. Sacramentalizing death on the battlefield elevates the moral dubiety of the killing process; making death a matter of honour cloaks with some higher purpose the production of death that is any army's utilitarian business. *Dulce et decorum est pro patria mori* — "It is sweet and seemly to die for ones country", wrote the poet Horace to sanctify the deaths of Roman legionnaires two thousand years ago. The lapidary phrase, "He sacrificed his life that others might live," links death on the battlefield with the sacrifices of religion.

A second purpose is to provide ritual and ceremony to help reinforce the bonding between soldiers and the submergence of self in the greater whole of the unit — be it platoon, company, regiment, or army. Evolved over many years, the military's ritual and rhythm of death — the slow march, the volley of shots, the playing of the last post, the monuments — are designed to separate the world of war and its denizens from the rest of humanity. Participating in the celebration of the soldier dead-in-war offers the living soldier a unique pattern of ceremony with its peculiar cadence of music and movement that strengthens the links between the comrades-in-arms still living.

A third purpose is to help the family of the dead soldier come to terms with the grief. Again, this has an instrumental function. The subconscious knowledge that the Army will help look after the wounds caused by the loss of a son, husband or father or daughter, wife and mother in the case of women soldiers is part of the deal that permits a soldier to go into battle. The military-promoted image, not inaccurate, of the Army as a kind of family brings with it the responsibility to help members of the family with the process of comprehending death. *Tout comprendre, c'est tout pardonner* is a French expression meaning "To understand everything is to forgive everything" and as the Army seeks to help grieving relatives understand their loss it simultaneously asks for forgiveness for the death that has taken place.

As we shall see with the Thompsons, it is precisely because the British Government has refused to provide the knowledge that would help them fully understand Lee's death, that they cannot yet begin the process of forgiving. But in the days and weeks after their son's death, the Army, within the limits of its traditions and its possibilities, did its very best to help Mick and Barbara and other members of the Thompson family cope with Lee's death.

Within a week of Lee's death, the letters began arriving at the Thompson's house in Coventry. Bill Hardy, a popular long-serving Labour councillor in Coventry and Lord Mayor in 1991 wrote on 28 February expressing "heartfelt condolences" on behalf of the "Citizens of Coventry."

> "The manifestation of war only serves to highlight man's inhumanity to man, and it is tragic that young men like Lee have to pay the ultimate sacrifice.
>
> Words are of little comfort at a time like this and it must be difficult for you to face a future that does not include your beloved Son, but please be assured that our prayers and thoughts are with you."

Two letters, both dated 4 March, express the difference between the way those who fought in the war and many of those who watched it on television reacted to Lee Thompson's death.

The Duke of Kent is Colonel-in-Chief of the Royal Regiment of Fusiliers. In the short, type-written letter there was a sentence which contained not only an error of fact but a sentiment that, while commonplace, struck a jarring note given the nature of the war that had just been fought.

After expressing his sorrow to learn of Lee's death, the Duke of Kent's letter went on:

> Whilst it must be an additional sadness to you that Lee was killed by an Allied airborne attack in very bad weather and visibility, you

From: H.R.H. The Duke of Kent, KG

York House
St. James's Palace
London S.W. 1

4th March, 1991

Dear Mr Thompson,

I was very saddened to learn of the death of your
son, Lee, whilst serving with the Third Battalion, Royal
Regiment of Fusiliers.

Whilst it must be an additional sadness to you
that Lee was killed by an Allied airborne attack in very
bad weather and visibility, you have the consolation of
knowing that he died on active service for his Queen and
country.

A senior officer of my Regiment will represent me
at Lee's funeral.

To you and your family I send my heartfelt
sympathy at this tragic time.

Yours sincerely,

Colonel in Chief
Royal Regiment of Fusiliers

M. Thompson, Esq

have the consolation of knowing that he died on active service for
his Queen and country.

This letter was to cause confusion amongst the parents of the
dead Fusiliers as they began talking to surviving soldiers and
found that the weather at the time of the attack was perfect. The
Duke of Kent launched the first in the series of false or partial
reports that led to an awareness amongst the parents of
inconsistency on the part of the authorities.

It was hardly the Duke's fault. He was doing his duty within
a traditional British order of things. A member of his staff would
have drafted the letter for the Duke's signature. The reference
to dying "for Queen and country", a time-honoured formula
from Victorian days, seemed curiously out of place. No other
letter of condolence used it. There were justifications for British
involvement in the Gulf War even if the restoration of the
despotic, decadent rule of the Kuwaiti royal family and the
continuing presence of Saddam Hussein as the ruler of Iraq
leave a sour taste in the mouths of those who felt that the war
was connected to a struggle for freedom or democracy, but is
difficult to see that the soldiers were fighting and were to die
for "Queen and country".

Critics of the war argued that the purpose was to strengthen
US and the West's domination in the region and in particular to
safeguard oil interests. Certainly, in the past ten years, some
sectors of the City and industry had made a great amount of
money from dealing with the dictatorships in the Gulf. British
diplomats had been obliged to humiliate themselves to Arab
dictators because of a television film about the vile treatment
of women in Arab states and there were repeated stories in the
press about the business affairs of Mrs Thatcher's son, Mark, in
the Gulf State of Oman.

World War Two ended with dictatorial forms of government
in Germany and Japan destroyed and democracy imposed on
the two countries by allied armies of occupation. In the more
recent example of the Falklands/Malvinas War, the restoration
of freedom in the islands led to the humiliation and collapse of
the military junta in Buenos Aires which, in turn, opened the
way to democratic freedoms in Argentina and elsewhere in Latin
America. Yet, the result twelve months after the Gulf War is
political stasis in the Gulf region and reinforced dictatorships
of a cruel and inhuman kind whether in Iraq, Saudi Arabia, Syria
or the Gulf Emirates themselves.

Standing up to the territorial ambitions of Saddam was necessary but the reluctance of all the European countries but France to commit ground troops suggests that the view of the Duke of Kent that this was a war for "Queen and country" was not one widely shared in other democratic countries.

The most important of the condolence letters that the Thompsons received was a lengthy hand-written one from Lieutenant Colonel Andrew De H Larpent, the commanding officer of Lee's battalion. Dated 4 March, six days after Lee's death, with the heading "Operation Granby", Lt. Col. Larpent wrote:

"I write to offer you my very sincere condolences over the so tragic death of your son Lee. The whole Battalion has been deeply affected by our losses and our thoughts over the past few days have been focussed on them and on you, their families. Over the past few months while we have been engaged on this great enterprise the whole Battalion has blended together into a closely knit group. We all knew that there would probably be casualties in battle and we prepared ourselves accordingly. That preparation helped but it does not remove the deep sense of pain and loss that we all feel. We are like a large family and we grieve like any family so please be assured that in your great loss you are not alone and we all feel as you do at this sad time.

There is no doubt that the allies were fortunate that casualties were so low overall. That is largely due to the excellent strategy of our leaders and to the extensive air campaign conducted so successfully by the US and allied air forces. That is why there is not bitterness here over what happened to us. I was close to the scene of the incident and we were in the midst of a battle at the time at the front of the Brigade. There was much confusion and it was just so tragic that two of our Warriors should have been hit in the way they were.

We are all very proud of those who have been taken from us. Lee was a fine young man and an excellent soldier. He and his colleagues that fell in battle died as soldiers in action and I can assure that they will never be forgotten.

I hope that we will get a chance to meet when we return and that you and your family will be able to attend the memorial events that will take place. To you and them I send my deepest sympathy on behalf of the whole Battalion."

Apart from the statement about there being "no bitterness" over the incident — a sentiment which may have reflected his own views as well as being officially prudent but which certainly did not sum up the feelings of Lee's comrades in C Company — Larpent's letter, written by someone who had been in the front line, was the best of the many that the Thompsons received from serving and retired soldiers.

Another letter came from Brigadier Christopher Hammerbeck, the commanding officer of the 4th Armoured Brigade. With his goofy-toothed smile, Hammerbeck emerged as one of the personalities of the war. His handwritten letter was a heartfelt expression of condolence but it contained several details which only added to the confusion that Lee's parents felt about exactly how and why their son had died.

> "I write with great sadness to express my condolences and sympathy to you about the death of Lee. To say that we were shocked and deeply upset is an understatement. I know that Lee's Commanding Officer will have written to you and described the circumstances of his death. He died displaying the greatest courage in attempting to rescue his comrades and his actions are in the greatest traditions of his distinguished regiment. His was an example of selflessness all too rare.
>
> My Brigade I know join me as one in sending you our sympathy over your loss. I am particularly saddened since I had promised them and myself that I could bring everyone home safely and I feel that I failed in this respect. The incident occurred during particularly confused fighting when it was difficult to define exactly where we and the enemy actually were...
>
> Please believe me when I say how sad I am for you and your family. You are in our thoughts and prayers at this sad time."

The Brigadier's warmly-written and well-intentioned letter contributed to Mick and Barbara Thompsons' perplexity. The letter from the Battalion's Commanding Officer, Lt. Col. Larpent, had not described the circumstances of Lee's death. To write of Lee's great courage and to raise the nature of his death to an act of military heroism was appreciated but soon enough it was to emerge that he had died in the back of a vehicle over which he had no control. To write of "particularly confused fighting when it was difficult to define exactly where we and the enemy actually were" jarred with the triumphant reports in all the media after the war's end which hailed both the air and ground campaign as being the most precisely-controlled deployment of military force in the history of warfare.

Other letters arrived from military leaders such as Lieutenant General Sir Peter de la Billiere, who commanded the British Forces in the Gulf War, from Sir David Craig, Marshall of the Royal Air Force and Chief of the Defence Staff, from General Sir Peter Inge, Commander-in-Chief of the British Army of the Rhine as well as from retired officers and soldiers. Each was couched in human terms, each regretted the "tragic mistake by one of our own Allied aircraft" and each letter reached out to the Thompsons to help them come to terms with their loss.

The British public responded. Dozens of letters from complete strangers arrived for the Thompsons at their house in Coventry. Women who had lost sons or husbands fighting in the Forces wrote to the Thompsons to express their sorrow. One morning after the news of Lee's death had been published, an elderly lady knocked on the door of the Thompson's house to hand in a bunch of flowers. Each letter has been kept in a plastic folder in a file, a testament to the decency of the British people when one of their own is ripped from their midst. The First World War poet Rupert Brooke defined the emotion that surrounds the death of an English soldier on service abroad.

> If I should die, think only this of me:
>   That there's some corner of a foreign field
> That is forever England. There shall be
>   In that rich earth a richer dust concealed;
> A dust whom England bore, shaped, made aware,
>   Gave, once, her flowers to love, her ways to roam,
> A body of England's, breathing English air,
>   Washed by the river, blest by suns of home.

The Regimental Chaplain, the Reverend Adrian Pollard, wrote about the service that was held on the day after the nine Fusiliers were killed

> The entire Battalion met in such a unified atmosphere of grief as I have never encountered. We heard Jesus's words of comfort to his followers in the Gospel of St. John; we said prayers for you and we sang "The Lord is my Shepherd". It is my hope and my prayer for you that each member of your family will be given real help and consolation through the services (that will be held) in memory of Lee.

The Army did more than write letters. Locally-based officers called on Mick and Barbara to offer their help. Services were held in Coventry and in Hemer, in northern Germany, where the Fusiliers were based. A simple memorial bearing the names of the nine dead men was unveiled in the presence of the relatives. Hand in hand, Mick and Barbara laid a wreath of pink flowers at their son's memorial. "It's lovely, just right," said Barbara in tears.

The efforts of the Army and the British public to support the parents of the nine young men killed in the Gulf were impressive and moving. But the soldiers were there because political leaders had decided they should take part in the fight. It was to be eight months before the Prime Minister, John Major, wrote a letter to the Thompsons expressing his sorrow. Eight months during which the Thompsons had been offered much sympathy. But they wanted and needed something more. The truth.

CHAPTER 6

The British Cover-Up

Watching the British establishment cover up its mistakes is a full-time job. In his book, *Freedom, the Individual and the Law*, the leading lawyer Geoffrey Robertson Q.C., has written that

> "No other Western democracy is so obsessed with keeping from the public information about its public servants, or so relentless in plumbing new legal depths to staunch leaks from its bureaucracy.
> "The cult of secrecy amongst our mandarins is not entirely explained by self-interest: there is a genuine belief that decisions are made better if made without publicity."

Nothing better underlines Robertson's observations than the continuing refusal of Whitehall to tell all that is known about the circumstances of Lee Thompson's death.

It was not until 23 July 1991, five months after the tragedy, that an official report was sent to the Thompsons. The letter accompanying the report was signed by a minor bureaucrat in the Ministry of Defence. To add what appeared to be indifference to incivility, the letter referred to Lee's death as having taken place on "26th January", a month before the actual day, and was addressed to "Mr P Thompson". The name of Lee's father is Mick.

Later, in the course of 1991, as Whitehall realized that the parents were not to be fobbed off with an extremely economical version of the truth, the Prime Minister, John Major, wrote to the Thompsons apologising both for the wrong date and the lack of the Defence Secretary's signature on the covering letter. Sent eight months after Lee's death John Major's condolences and his apology for the style of his Defence Secretary were too late. The lack of civility from the Government which had gained considerable political prestige from the war in which Lee had died worsened the feeling of the parents and made them all the more determined to get at the truth.

In the end, these were not deliberate but rather minor administrative mistakes, even if they were deeply hurtful to the family. But when Whitehall starts to cover up some subconscious mechanism in the system starts to emit signals, mini-errors, which alert the experienced watcher to the process of dissimulation about to begin.

"The letter upset us, but it was the fact that the report didn't tell us what really happened that was the worse," recalls Mick Thompson.

The report accompanying the Ministry of Defence letter in July 1991 was not in fact the report of the Board of Inquiry. That report has not been published in full, and in particular, the evidence given to the Board remains a Whitehall secret. What was sent to the Thompsons was a text of what was read out in Parliament. We shall analyze this text below but in the covering letter the Government began emitting its own smoke-screen to confuse and dismay the Thompsons still further.

After admitting, contrary to earlier reports, that the incident happened in "clear" weather and that "C Company was stationary after earlier fighting", the Ministry of Defence letter went on

> The Board concluded that 3 Royal Regiment of Fusiliers was in no way to blame for the incident. All its vehicles were correctly displaying the inverted "V" and fluorescent panels. It is clear that the two Warriors were attacked by two USAF A-10 aircraft, which should have attacked Iraqi armour more than 20 kilometres to the east of C Company's position. The pilots said that they identified their target from a description given to them by aircraft who had previously attacked the correct target.
>
> There is a conflict of evidence between the pilots of the aircraft and the British Assistant Divisional Air Liason Officer (DALO) about whether the pilots were given the grid reference for the Iraqi target. The Board has recommended that procedures should be tightened up to ensure that the co-ordinates for a target are always given to and acknowledged by the aircraft pilot.
>
> In spite of all our efforts, the Board could not resolve the conflict of evidence over why the aircraft were in the wrong place and why the two Warrior vehicles were misidentified. It is clear that all UK and USAF personnel were striving to achieve their individual tasks. Given the understandable pressure of events on all those involved, it is inevitable that, at some stage, difficulties may arise.

The use of the word "difficulties" to describe the death of nine people may be put down to civil service training but the letter and attached report to be read out in Parliament raised more questions than it answered.

The Ministry of Defence was emphatic that the soldiers were "in no way to blame for the incident." But, having raised the issue of blame, the Government was not prepared to attribute it. Instead, there was "a conflict of evidence" between what the A-10 pilots had said and what the British Air Liason officer said. As we have seen, the heavily-censored evidence from the American side, which emerged after persistent attempts by the parents, was even more damning as the pilots claimed that the British Warriors did not carry any identification marks visible to close examination by binoculars from the aircraft cockpit.

But at least the Americans offered statements and records of communications between US military personnel. On the British side, no evidence was made available to the parents so that they, not Whitehall, could decide who was approaching a description of the truth.

To read the report made to Parliament (not, it is necessary to stress the same as the Board of Inquiry's report which is still covered by Whitehall secrecy) is to enter a world in which everyone has done his duty, everyone has followed orders, and everything "was in accordance with established procedures". There was "no blame and responsibility" for either the Fusiliers, or for the British Assistant Divisional Air Liason Officer and, finally,

> the Board did not establish whether the USAF personnel involved were at fault. It was clearly established that the USAF A-10s delivered the missiles, but the Board could not establish precisely why they attacked the wrong target.

The reply is a classic of Whitehall obfuscation. Nobody was at fault, and even if it appeared that fault lay with the pilots they were nonetheless not really to blame.

This lies at the heart of the parents' concern. A limited set of conclusions was made available from the Ministry of Defence but the evidence, the interviews, the documents, the signals, the recordings of voice traffic and details of the cross-examination of the witnesses at the Board of Inquiry remain a secret.

Mick and Barbara Thompson and the other parents were (and are) not allowed themselves to examine the information in the Government's possession and come to their own conclusions sufficient at last to answer the question that haunts them: how and why did their son die? Instead, the Government treated them as children unfit to handle information that remains the property of the state.

From early on, the parents felt that the cover-up was due, in part, to diplomatic reasons. Mel Gillespie from Tynemouth who lost his 19-year-old son, Richard, in the attack told the *Daily Mirror* in May, 1991: "This blunder may be an embarrassment to Anglo-American relations but that is no reason to sweep the truth under the carpet." After the Government report was made to Parliament in July 1991, Mick Thompson expressed his doubts:

> Lee's death had to show negligence on somebody's part and clearly the Americans were to blame. So why haven't they said so? I think it's a whitewash — a cover-up to save Anglo-American relations.

The United States and the United Kingdom of Great Britain and Northern Ireland do indeed have a peculiar relationship which is unlike any other between two sovereign states. It covers political, economic, diplomatic, and military relations. The British embassy in Washington is the biggest embassy of any foreign power in the United States. Britain provides a home to numerous American military bases. Normally when troops from a foreign country are stationed abroad there is a treaty agreed between the two countries defining the rights and role of the foreign military bases. But this is not the case in Britain. The term "special relationship" was developed after World War Two to define this peculiar connection between the two countries. Christopher Hitchens, the British writer who lives in Washington, has written a book examining Anglo-American relations called *Blood, Class and Nostalgia.* In it he writes

> The 'special relationship' is something that is *supposed* to elude definition; *supposed* to be protean and vague. It was not even given a name until Winston Churchill sought to encapsulate it, for now forgotten short-term reasons, in 1946. It is neither a political alliance, a strategic consensus, an ethnic coalition, nor a cultural and linguistic condominium — yet it is all of these.

The relationship between England and America is thus impossible to define but nevertheless deeply affects dealings between the two countries especially in the area of military policy and activity. The British Government has been the strongest in resisting any proposals for a shift to a European-centred defence policy. When America beckons, the English jump to attention. In 1985, American bombers used Britain as a base to bomb Tripoli in their unsuccessful attempt to assassinate

Colonel Gaddafi. Spain, Greece and the Philippines all have US bases in their countries but the American military presence there is regulated by legal treaties between governments, and, after due negotiations between the two governments, has just ended in the Philippines for example. In Britain, by contrast, American servicemen are literally above the law and cannot be tried by British courts for offences committed against British citizens. When Iraq invaded Kuwait, Britain at once sent forces to fight alongside the Americans.

The special relationship is far more important to Britain than to America. In the United States, the part played by British (or French) forces in the Gulf War barely rated a mention in the daily accounts in the American television and press which were manipulated, almost entirely controlled by the Pentagon. Britain's contribution was welcomed of course but far more media attention was paid to the activities of the pilots or troops from Arab countries. America simply took — and takes — Britain for granted, whereas the presence of Arab military forces in alliance with the United States was of far greater diplomatic and symbolic weight in a region where a main aim of US policy was to break up the anti-Israel front of the Arab dictatorships.

To be critical of the special relationship, which in Hitchens' words is "a hypocritical and unequal agreement which is both covert and uncodified. The British, of course, delight to conduct foreign policy in this way", is not to relapse into a crude anti-Americanism, which in many ways is a contemporary "socialism of fools". The service of the United States in defending democracy and resisting totalitarianism in the mid-20th century is well enough known. But not every decision the United States takes is wise, and the role of an ally is not automatically to go along with every whim and desire of the dominant partner. But the existence of the "special relationship" makes it all but impossible for British officials — political, military, or diplomatic — to deal with their opposite numbers in the United States with openness and a clear view of where British interests lie. In the case of the Gulf friendly fire victims, there is no evidence that the British exerted any effective pressure on the United States, neither at the time of the incident nor in the months since, to report fully and clearly on what happened. The fact that the tragedy involved the Americans allowed the British penchant for secrecy and covering-up to be further reinforced in the name of not disturbing the "special relationship." It is difficult to imagine that if, say, Saudi or French jets had killed the nine soliders, the Government would have been quite so ready to issue its 'No one is to blame' report.

Already, within a month of Lee 's death, Mick and Barbara knew that their son had been killed unnecessarily because of a major cock-up. The Fusiliers they had met had expressed bitterness and anger over what happened. They told the parents that the visibility was fine, the Warriors were marked with giant inverted "V's", about six feet across and had bright green and orange fluorescent plastic sheets tied to the roof of the vehicles. As we have seen, the identification system had been ordered by the Americans after there had been confusion over identifying allied vehicles in the Battle for Khafji late in January. They heard that the A-10 planes, the famous "Tankbusters", ungainly slow jets designed to fight with armoured divisions by acting as airborne anti-tank missile and cannon platforms, had swooped low and after shooting their rockets had waggled their wings in a "V for Victory" sign before going off.

Obvious questions were there to be asked. How could the A-10 pilots, supposedly the hottest of hot shots in vehicle recognition, mistake for advancing Iraqi T 54/55 tanks stationary allied personnel carriers carrying American imposed identification marks and situated exactly where they were meant to be according to the plan of attack?

And if the American pilots did think they were Iraqi armour on its way to attack allied troops why did they fire only one Maverick each before disappearing? Why had the pilots not read back the exact grid reference of the target they proposed to attack so that it could be confirmed by the British forward air controller?

These questions were not obsessions of the Thompsons alone. In Tynemouth, in Rochdale, in Rye Harbour, in County Durham, other families whose teenage sons had been killed wanted to know how and why. The eleven soldiers wounded in the incident, some of them still undergoing hospital treatment months later, also wanted to know who was responsible.

It was an ache that grew as time passed. The corporals and captains who escorted them around from service to service could provide no answer. The parents heard different rumours. But an official explanation of what happened was not the Army's duty. That obligation belonged to the people who had sent Lee Thompson out to the Gulf — Her Majesty's Government.

Since Lee's death there had been a puzzle in the Thompsons' mind. In the immediate aftermath, they received condolence letters from the Lord Mayor of Coventry and their local MP but nothing from the government. They had questions they wanted answering. They wrote to Neil Kinnock who quickly replied as did Martin O'Neill, Labour's Defence spokesperson, who wrote to the government asking what was going on.

A letter from the Thompsons to Tom King, the Defence Secretary, went unanswered until they approached him directly at the welcome home parade held by the City of London. At the end of June, King wrote a condolence letter and told them: "We are investigating very fully the circumstances surrounding your son's tragic death. There are many aspects that need to be covered and much information to be collected."

What the Thompsons were not told was that Whitehall was locked in what for government bureaucrats was their equivalent of mortal combat with Washington over what had happened. And, as in the Gulf War, the Americans were to emerge as the easy winners.

Put simply, the Americans blamed the British while the British were convinced that the Americans were responsible. At this stage of their quest for the truth, the Thompsons — and the reporters who had been tracking the story — entered that most private of worlds in Britain, that ring-fenced by the establishment-defined need for secrecy.

Officers and Ministry of Defence officials would say nothing on the record but the stench of a scandal was seeping out. "The British had thrown back the American report," said one source but it was clear that the Americans were not to be moved from the view expressed by Lieutenant General Chuck Horner, the commander of the air forces in the Gulf that "the British air controller had been responsible."

The report was carefully filed in the cupboard in the Thompson's house which was now filling up with letters and documents linked to Lee's death.

Barbara Thompson carefully composed her own letters in a reporter's notebook before writing them out in fair to send off.

Now she sent her first letter to President Bush. She asked the questions that all parents wanted answered. Why were the A-10s where they were? Why did they only fire a missile apiece before leaving? What was the rank of the officers? How did they fail to see the identification marks on the British Warriors?

As the accusations of a cover-up began to be made public, the Government tried to persuade the families to drop their pressure for the truth. A trip was hastily arranged to the United States, paid for by anonymous American "well-wishers" and by

British Airways, whose chairman, Lord King, was one of the biggest corporate contributors to the ruling Conservative Party's funds in the 1980s. The Thompsons refused to go but the eight other families accepted, hoping that in seeing President Bush, they would get from him the truth that had been denied them by their own Government. In a biting editorial, the *Coventry Evening Telegraph* condemned the motives behind the offer of the all-expenses-paid trip. Under the heading, *Holiday not the Answer*, the paper gave its view:

"Bereaved parents Mick and Barbara Thompson are deep in mourning for the loss of their beloved son Lee, killed by American 'friendly fire' in the Gulf War. The pain showed as they travelled bravely to Germany for an Army memorial service and it is biting deep and hard today as they refuse a misplaced offer of solace.

A holiday in the United States with a sunshine trip to Hawaii and the promise of a meeting with President Bush is not the way to wash away the grief or the anger they feel at the shabby cover-up enquiry into their son's death.

The all-expenses-paid offer by American well wishers is in incredibly bad taste. No matter how well-intentioned the plan, those behind it should realise that no public relations exercise is going to expunge the guilt.

This holiday-in-the-sun is going to help no one, except perhaps those who feel the need to throw a blanket over a nation's costly mistake. It will not comfort Mr and Mrs Thompson.

They need the American and British governments to tell them what really happened in the few, horrific moments leading to the death of their son and his eight young friends."

The *Coventry Evening Telegraph* had hit the nail on the head. One of its reporters, Claire White, had covered the story of the Thompsons as they moved from being the centre of media attention in the city as parents of the dead Fusilier to becoming two local citizens setting out to persuade their government to tell them the truth. "She's been absolutely smashing, one of the family," says Barbara Thompson about the journalist, Claire White. At each development, the young reporter had gone round to discuss with the Thompsons and get their views. She persistently phoned up Whitehall and the White House to try and obtain more details.

Sometimes, regional newspapers are looked down upon as the poor relations of the national newspapers produced in London. But for most of 1991, there was a major story concerning a government cover-up linked to one of the biggest events in recent history, the Gulf War, and it had been local papers such as the *Coventry Evening Telegraph* which had covered it, and written important editorials in defence of citizens' rights while the big guns of what used to be Fleet Street had been strangely silent. (To be fair, *The Independent*, the *Guardian* and the *Daily Mail* had all carried news reports and features about the parents' belief they were not being told the full truth but by early January 1992, no national newspaper had seen fit to launch a campaign for the truth, nor to thunder criticisms in its editorials against the Whitehall cover-up.)

The news of the offer of a free trip to the United States spurred one Coventry citizen, Mr B.C. Moore, to write to the *Evening Telegraph* thus:

> "As an ex-serviceman I must write about the recent free trip to the USA offered to the bereaved relatives of those killed in the 'friendly fire' incident in the Gulf War.
>
> The 'well-wisher' funding this trip is most probably the American government and I see this as an offer of sympathy in an attempted whitewash.
>
> I can fully understand Mrs Barbara Thompson's anger that no one will take the blame for her son's death. Unfortunately, she is up against the establishment and this is a real hard nut to crack, embracing diplomatic relations, trade, money etc.
>
> Regrettably, these are far more important to the people concerned than the tragic loss of life of a soldier and his comrades.
>
> Your correspondent E.R. Cooke says that apportioning the blame to individuals will not soften the blow. True, but at least Lee's parents would know who was responsible for his death. That is only right."

As it was, the parents' trip in September 1991 nearly turned into a public relations disaster as the British families were housed in a hotel in Washington at the same time as the hotel hosted an annual US Air Force show. On the floors below the lobby and coffee shop areas were graphic displays of the technology and weaponry that had killed their sons. If any of the carefully shepherded parents had poked a nose into what was happening elsewhere in the hotel or asked a few questions they might well have found out, at least informally and on an off-the-record basis, what had happened to their sons. Instead, British embassy staff were constantly in attendance to make sure the parents, tired and jet-lagged after their transatlantic trip, were under surveillance at all times.

Although Mick and Barbara Thompson refused to participate in what they felt was a cynical attempt by the British Government and its supporters to show concern, they were glad that some of the other mothers and fathers they had got to know would meet President Bush face to face in the White House and ask for the truth to be revealed.

Barbara Thompson had already written twice to the American President, without getting an acknowledgement, let alone a reply to her letters. Now she opened her notebook one more time and composed a letter for one of the other parents to deliver in person to President Bush.

> Mr President:
> This is the third time I have written to you. We have not had an answer from our two previous letters — whether you have received them I do not know — so I have asked Mr and Mrs Atkinson whose son Paul was murdered with our son Lee and seven more comrades in the A-10 incident in the Gulf War.
> We are far from satisfied with the outcome of the inquiry into the incident. It is clear to us that the pilot was to blame for the very grave error that he made. Here are questions we would like to ask the pilot.
> 1) Why couldn't he tell the difference between a Warrior Personnel Carrier and T 54/55 Iraqi tanks from 8,000 feet with high powered binoculars?
> 2) Why, if he thought they were Iraqi tanks, did he only take two from the centre of the formation and not the whole line of them?
> 3) Was he given a drug test *after* the mission?
> 4) Why is it reported in the newspaper that he is back on flying duties but still receiving counselling. Was he another rambo who wanted another notch on his gun?
> We know accidents happen in wartime, but with all the high-tech equipment you proudly brag about why is it left to an incompetent pilot to use it?
> We are very bitter that you won't accept responsibility for one of your pilots. We don't wish to know his name, but a personal letter of condolence from yourself to nine bereaved families, might have helped us a little at the time of our loss.
> Hoping you will find time to reply to our letter.
> Yours disillusioned,
> Mick and Barbara Thompson.

The Thompsons are still waiting for a reply. President Bush, it appears, is too important a man to write explaining why his planes killed Lee Thompson.

Other parents who returned home from Washington also felt let down by the American leader. In direct conversation with one father, Mel Gillespie, President Bush declared that "the information was freely available to anyone who requested it." President Bush, himself a pilot who was shot down in the Pacific War (though some war historians have argued that Bush bailed out early leaving the gunner sitting behind him in the cockpit to plunge to his death whereas with more prudent piloting it would have been possible to land the plane and save both lives), entered into a heated exchange with Pete Atkinson of County Durham, whose son, Paul, was one of the nine British soldiers killed by the Americans in the Gulf. According to Pete Atkinson

> I asked Bush why their pilots hadn't followed procedures and were off course at the time. Bush turned on me and said: 'Did you (i.e. the British) follow procedures?'
>
> When I said our report said we did, he got really angry and said: 'You want the facts? You'll get the facts.' Then I was told we would have the American report before we left — but nothing happened.

The parents left the White House with the expectation that, at last, the truth about what happened on 26 February would be made available to them. But British officials quickly got to work to ensure the offical Whitehall line was followed — there would be no full report and the parents would have to make do with the sanitized, incomplete version they had already been given. In response to newspaper enquiries the British embassy in Washington denied that President Bush had agreed to release the details of the US investigation into the incident. The parents believed that Bush had promised them a copy of the US report before they left the United States to return to Britain. But this promise was not to be kept. A White House spokesperson told *Coventry Evening Telegraph* reporter, Claire White, that the process of preparing an American report for forwarding to the parents via the British ambassador would take some time. With an ambiguous choice of words the White House spokesperson added: "They're working very carefully because they want to get the facts right for the relatives."

As autumn came the Thompsons were still waiting for the American version of what happened. Unlike secrecy-obsessed Britain, the United States has a Freedom of Information Act which allows far greater access for American citizens, and foreigners, to US Administration documents. (As a writer who has worked in America, I have found Americans much more open and more free with information than their British counterparts. Our country suffers from a fear of telling the citizen what is happening, a secrecy that goes beyond Government and infects (and highly suits) business, the police and most public institutions. Libel laws are used by the rich and powerful to silence criticism and inquiry. At least two respected American current affairs magazines, the *New Republic* and the

Nation cannot go on sale in England because of libel cases issued within English jurisdiction against the papers.)

American openness has its limits however. The Freedom of Information Act allows the exclusion of material which might cause diplomatic damage to America's allies. Historians who read through 50-year-old reports sent from the US embassy in London which are freely available in the National Archives building in Washington D.C. come across curious white slips of paper which are inserted at regular intervals in the archive files. The paper informs the researcher that the document has been removed at the request of a foreign government which feared it might do damage to relations with the United States. What is really meant is that the document might expose some long-forgotten chicanery by the British authorities. So the British Government sends her weeders to do their work in the US historical archives to make sure that even events now long dead in history remain covered up.

We shall look at the American evidence inasmuch as it has been revealed to the parents in the next chapter but the crucial decision had already been taken in Whitehall which was to publish and say nothing that reflected badly on the Americans. The Thompsons are British, not American citizens and it is to their government that they look for support, not rejection, in their quest for the truth.

Once again, Barbara Thompson got out her reporters' notebook and drafted another letter, dated 2 October 1991 and addressed to John Major.

"We are the parents of Fusilier Lee Thompson. He was one of the British servicemen killed by the A-10 pilot in the Gulf War incident.

To put it mildly we are totally appalled by the response we have received from all our letters we have sent to Tom King who in our opinion isn't a fit person to be your defence secretary.

All of the families said he would send the inquiry report out to us prior to the summer recess, and we were right. He thought we would all go away and forget, but, by God, he was wrong. We are more determined than ever now.

When the other eight families went to the USA, George Bush promised them they would receive a copy of the US report into the incident but so far we have had nothing.

Is this being blocked by the MoD? Is there a big cover-up to protect someone high in military office and not just a pilot who is at fault?

It is a disgrace that we should have to wait so long to get to know the truth but I can assure you we will continue to pursue this matter. All we want is the truth so we can have peace of mind.

We do accept accidents happen in wartime during difficult circumstances but this wasn't one of them.

We would have had no complaints whatsoever if our son lost his life to the enemy. But the way he did we will never understand why unless we are told the truth that is *all* we are asking for.

Surely your being a father, you can understand that."

On 13 November 1991, the Prime Minister replied to the Thompsons. "There is no question of anyone concealing information or covering anything up," he wrote. Apart from the tautology, the reference to a cover-up, the first time any British minister had used the term, was beginning to show the extent to which the Government was being rattled by the parents' continuing insistence that the full truth be revealed.

Major was unable to reveal anything new save a curious statement "that the degree of details of ground objects visible from the air can critically depend on the line of sight in relation to the sun."

The Thompsons puzzled over this new clue. "Beware the Hun from the Sun" was a staple of anyone brought up on a diet of Biggles and Rockfist Rogan in the 1940s and 1950s but since they were denied all the other details of the angle from which the A-10s had attacked, it was impossible to know whether a momentary touch of sun-blindness had justified letting loose the Mavericks on the British troops.

Neither Mr Major's intervention, nor a letter of condolence from the Queen, which arrived a few weeks later, did anything to soothe the parents. They gave the details to their local MP, John Hughes, who raised all the parents' questions in an adjournment debate in the House of Commons in December, 1991. He received a brush-off from the junior defence minister, Lord Archie Hamilton. The government's ranks, it seemed, were closed.

But the Thompsons refused to give in. Their house had become a shrine to their dead son but also a nerve centre of a campaign to find the truth. Together with other parents they put up some money to pay the expenses of solicitors so that they could be represented legally at the inquest which had yet to be held by the Coroner in Oxford under whose jurisdiction it fell as the bodies were brought back to Brize Norton.

In their BBC publications book, *All Necessary Means. Inside the Gulf War*, two BBC reporters, Ben Brown and David Shukman, revealed that during the war a special committee had been set up under the cabinet minister John Wakeham "to prepare for all conceivable public relations pitfalls" including "how coroners' inquests would be handled." So far, requests by the parents to have the information in the hands of the Oxford Coroner, who by the beginning of 1992 had still not announced a date for the inquest, had been in vain.

A committee was formed to help the Thompsons and work was carried out in Germany and Washington to dig up background on the incident. An investigative team from the BBC 2 programme, *Taking Liberties*, was compiling its own report for transmission on the anniversary of Lee Thompson's death.

Somewhere exist at least three men, the two A-10 pilots and the British DALO, who can tell exactly what happened. They are unlikely to come forward, at least for the time being. But the civil servants in the British and American governments are sitting on documents which could take the Thompsons much closer to the truth than they have been permitted so far.

Their story is a small one perhaps in the epic military exercise that took place twelve months ago. According to one contributor to *Jane's Intelligence Review*, "in real terms, Desert Storm was not a war" but Mick Thompson still believes that it was right for Britain to send troops to help dislodge Saddam Hussein and he is proud of his son doing his duty as a soldier.

Their anger is not against the Army but against the Government that will not afford them a centuries old British right — that of knowing how and why a violent death took place.

CHAPTER 7

A Conflict of Evidence

In Chapter Four, we left the A-10 pilots as they flew away from the scene of the disaster. If they had genuinely believed that they had successfully attacked Iraqi T 54/55 tanks, their elation did not last long.

In his account of what happened (as far as it can be ascertained from the parliamentary report based on the Army's Board of Inquiry), the British ground controller told a different story. At the time, around 2.30 p.m. on Tuesday 26 February when the A-10s were passed on to him in the hope he could find them a target to shoot at, his interest lay in the attack being conducted by Britain's 7th Armoured Brigade operating to the north of the 4th Armoured Brigade and pushing on hard eastwards to the Wadi Al Batin which marked the border between Iraq and Kuwait.

Here it was a question of attacking Iraqi tanks as well as defensive positions, in contrast to the task of the 4th Brigade to the south which was dealing mainly with artillery emplacements. The US Air Force had sent in two missions to attack Iraqi armour on behalf of the 7th Armoured Brigade. The fighting was taking place about twenty kilometres east and slightly north of where the Fusiliers were resting after securing the gun emplacements.

According to the British account, the Divisional Air Liason Officer (DALO) passed on the same grid reference to the two A-10 pilots who were looking for something to do as he had given to the previous US Air Force planes which had successfully attacked Iraqi armour on behalf of the British ground forces.

The A-10 pilots, as we have seen, deny that they received these grid references and in their reports said they decided they were in an area occupied only by Iraqis on the basis of a description given to them by an F-16 pilot and by the assurance from the DALO that there were no "friendlies" within 10 kilometres. The A-10 pilots themselves decided which target to attack on the basis of their own identification of the vehicles they saw as Iraqi tanks.

There is a further confusion in that the DALO told the Board of Inquiry that he had given a code word at the same time as he gave the correct grid references for the enemy armour he wanted to attack. The use of the code word was needed so that the allied pilots could be clear that they were receiving instructions from friendly controllers, and not the Iraqis. Whether the Iraqis were sophisticated enough or could lay their hands on people able to imitate and transmit to perfection the slangy, jargonized exchanges in American or English accents sufficient to fool allied pilots is an open question. Certainly, the A-10 pilots denied strongly ever having been informed of the code word and knowing of its relevance.

The code word question may be a red herring as the basic conflict lies in whether the DALO did transmit the correct grid reference or not. Either he or the A-10 pilots are lying. It would be pleasant to write the problem off as a confusion rising from the fog of war but there really can only be one set of facts corresponding to what happened, to the truth.

Either the DALO did transmit the correct grid reference for the attack, which the A-10s INS navigation system could have instantly told the pilots that they were in the wrong place, or he did not and the only information he gave them was that there were no friendly forces in the area they were over-flying.

However, and it is an important point, even if the DALO had not transmitted the correct grid reference, there remains the fundamental error of the pilots in misidentifying the Warriors for Iraqi tanks. Immediately after the attack, when the A-10 pilots communicated to the DALO the grid reference of the target they had attacked, the British officer realised something disastrously wrong had occurred. He called up a US reconnaisance flight which, in the words of the British report, "reported that fluorescent air recognition panels could be seen from 6,000 feet and the type of vehicles could be identified from 14,000 feet."

As the Americans sought to justify what had happened they reached out for any excuse. US Marine Corps Major General Bob Johnstone, Chief of Staff of the US Army's Central Command which had fought the war, wrote to Air Marshall Sir John Kemball in June 1991 as the British military put pressure on their American colleagues to come clean. General Johnstone argued that the identification signs had become covered over, "the weather earlier in the day was poor, and dust could have

UNITED STATES CENTRAL COMMAND
OFFICE OF THE DEPUTY COMMANDER IN CHIEF AND CHIEF OF STAFF
MACDILL AIR FORCE BASE, FLORIDA 33608-7001

10 July 1991

Air Marshal Sir John Kemball KCB CBE BA RAF
Headquarters Strike Command
Royal Air Force
High Wycombe
Buckinghamshire
United Kingdom

Dear Air Marshal Kemball,

Since speaking with you last, I have sent you the statements
of ▆▆▆▆▆▆▆▆▆▆▆▆▆▆▆ and ▆▆▆▆▆▆▆▆▆▆▆▆▆▆▆▆▆▆,
the A-10 pilots involved in the fratricide with the British
Warrior Infantry Fighting Vehicles. I have also received a
message from the Commander, ▆▆▆▆▆▆▆▆▆▆▆▆▆▆▆clarifying
the apparent differences between the statement attributed to the
pilots in my 6 June letter and in their original statements.

As you will see from the pilots' statements and as verified
in the message from their Wing Commander, the pilots state they
do not recall that target coordinates were given prior to their
attack. These statements are consistent with their original
statement after the incident.   When interviewed in late May,
they implied they were passed grid position▆▆▆▆ This
statement was subsequently clarified to mean they derived that
position from their inertial system after overflying the target
described by ▆▆▆▆▆ (on station F-16 flight) and after being
told by ▆▆▆▆▆ (British DALO) that no friendlies were within 10
kilometers. Both pilots stated they do not recall any reference
to ▆▆▆▆▆ or grid position ▆▆▆during the mission.

In response to your question about the mission and tasking
of the A-10 flight, both aircraft were a scheduled close air
support event tasked to check in with an ABCCC airborne
controller for specific tasking. The pilots were directed to a
contact point in ▆▆▆ but were unable to work that area due to
poor weather. They were redirected to contact the Air Support
Operations Center (ASOC) who subsequently redirected them to
position ▆▆▆and advised them to contact ▆▆▆▆▆for tasking.
▆▆▆▆▆told the A-10 flight to continue to position ▆▆▆at
which time ▆▆▆▆▆came up on frequency to pass information
about the target. The A-10 pilots correlated this information
with what they saw on the ground to verify their target position.

under flight lead (autonomous) control and not under direct control of the DALO. The aircraft were cleared to engage targets in an area, but were not within visual contact of a controller. Regrettably, the positional discrepancy led to the engagement of the IFV.

Another causal factor of this incident was the failure of our recognition system to ensure identification of friendly vehicles. Your units reported their ▮▮▮▮▮▮▮▮▮▮▮ were installed and visible during a reconnaissance flight over the area subsequent to the incident. The A-10 pilots state they made two dry identification passes, using binoculars, prior to engagement, and that from their 8,000 ft altitude ▮▮▮▮▮▮▮ ▮▮▮▮▮▮▮▮▮▮ were not visible. Although the weather at the time of the incident was good, the weather earlier in the day was poor, and dust could have resulted in recognition features which were obscured. ▮▮▮▮▮▮▮▮▮▮▮▮▮▮▮▮▮▮▮▮ served us well during Desert Storm, but obviously failed at this critical time. An electronic means of identification friend or foe may have prevented this tragic incident and development and incorporation of such a system is one of the recommendations we have submitted in our lessons learned.

I have tried to stick to the facts and avoid opinion in responding to your inquiry. Although I agree with most of the findings of your incident board, I am not sure the finding in paragraph 16 is valid. Perhaps air planning and air control were in accordance with established procedures, but I believe there was a failure by both the ground controller and the pilots to ensure a thorough brief and understanding of the situation and environment. This opinion is not meant to cast dispersions on either side, however, they both were operating at a hectic combat pace on a rapidly changing battlefield where the fog of war is inevitable at some point. Many factors and misunderstandings led them down the primrose path, but the bottom line is they were not on the same sheet of music and that led to disaster.

We can certainly understand the interest and concern of the Government of the United Kingdom and the Royal Air Force in fully investigating this incident and in reviewing procedures to eliminate future fratricide incidents. We share that concern, however, we believe there is little to be gained by further investigating this particular incident. I can ensure you we have thoroughly reviewed it, learned valuable lessons, and taken action to prevent fratricide in the future. Nothing can bring back the lives of your brave soldiers or ease the sorrow of their families, but hopefully the attention given to this incident will result in saving lives in future conflicts.

Bob Johnston

R. B. JOHNSTON
Major General, USMC
Deputy Commander

resulted in recognition features which were obscured." It is acceptable perhaps to believe that one, two, perhaps several of the Warriors had somehow managed to dirty themselves to such an extent that the thick black Vs on their sides and roof were obscure. It is possible that some of the fluorescent sheets had been carried off in the wind and rain. But it is stretching credulity too far to say that all 37 vehicles operating in C Company had had their identification marks obscured. The Americans have a rejoinder to people like General Johnstone who recount such stories — "Go and tell it to the Marines!"

The loquacious Lieutenant-General Chuck Horner, the US Air Force commander in the Gulf War, was more honest when he was interviewed by two BBC correspondents, Ben Brown and David Shukman, for their book, *All Necessary Means. Inside the Gulf War.* They taxed him on the friendly fire incident and the failure of the pilots to see the markings. "He asked us whether if he drove through 10 kilometres of dust, for example, he would have the correct markings. 'Yes, if I'm driving the vehicle,' he said, 'no, if I'm looking for it.'"

This Delphic utterance is the closest the Americans have come to admitting that perhaps their pilots were eager, over-eager, to find a target. But overall, General Horner continues to insist that the British were to blame. He has gone on the record twice to that effect though he has refused — apparently on order from US Chief of Staff, Colin Powell, to be interviewed by the BBC2 programme, *Taking Liberties*, when its producers requested an interview with him. He also rejected a request I faxed to him that he meet with the Thompsons and explain to them, face to face, his version of what happened.

His views however are clear enough about the 'blue-on-blue', a US military expression for killing one of their own, involving the Fusiliers. According to Brown and Shukman, who interviewed Horner, "Lieutenant-General Chuck Horner claimed that the British air controller had been responsible." In the official journal of the US Air Force, the *Air Force Magazine*, published in June 1991, Horner was even more forthright. Describing different friendly fire incidents involving Americans, Horner continued

> Then we had an A-10 hit a British vehicle. In that case, it was a failure of command and control. The forward air controller was a British guy. The (US planes) had taken off, and they came on station. They were cleared to a crossroads with a police station or a border post or something.

So the FAC cleared them, and he said, "We do not have any (friendly) forces within 4,000 meters, four kilometers of your location." So the US pilots saw this column in the north coming in, and they shot at them. In fact, it was British people.

The fundamental system is the support coordination line. It is generally out to about the limit of (friendly) artillery. Anything inside that line has to be controlled by a forward air controller. That is how the pilot operates. He can't drop (ordnance) unless he's cleared by a forward air controller, except in an emergency. Outside the fire support coordination line, the flight leader is allowed to attack any target within the general rules of engagement.

So it is clear that in the view of the US Air Force commander, both in general cases and in the specific case of the Fusiliers, the responsibility for attacks within fifteen miles of friendly army positions lies with the army controller on the ground.

But in the same interview Horner acknowledged that after the friendly fire deaths during the Battle of Khafji, the Americans had a problem. 25 per cent of all American casualties in the Gulf War were caused by friendly fire. Because the overall figure of allied troops lost was so low, the numbers appear small. But if, say, 1,000 soldiers had lost their lives and 250 of them had been killed by their own side then the self-satisfaction exuding from the Gulf generals would have been evaporated by the anger of public opinion. The plain fact is that the Americans had not thought through or made adequate preparations for helicopters and planes attacking their own side. Horner admits the problem candidly:

After Khafji, we realized it was an extremely difficult task. A lot of these systems like Lantern and Maverick are relatively new to the inventory, so we don't have a lot of experience practising these devices in joint exercises. When the war started, we looked at putting things like infrared flashes and stuff like that on vehicles. We never really got a chance to develop additional measures like that.

The main thing we did was to talk to the guys and say, "If in doubt, don't drop."

So again, we are brought back to the question of why the A-10 pilots did "drop" their missiles on the Fusiliers. The DALO says he gave them a correct grid reference. They say all they got from the DALO was clearance that there were no friendly forces about.

Even if we leave this conflict of evidence (in this instance a euphemism for one person telling the truth and the other lying) to one side for the moment, there remains the crucial question of why did the A-10 pilots attack a stationary group of British armoured personnel carriers which were carrying allied identification marks designed to be seen from the air and which, apart from being tracked vehicles, were unlike the T 54/55 tanks the A-10 pilots claimed they were blasting?

Some evidence on what may have happened comes from the one case of friendly fire in the Gulf War in which the pilot responsible was named. He was Lt. Col. Ralph Hayes who flew an Apache helicopter which destroyed two US Army Bradley armoured personnel carriers, killing two US soldiers on 27 February. Lt. Col. Hayes was the only pilot responsible for a friendly fire incident whose name became known. He has left the US Army and was interviewed at length on American television.

Britain's Sky News programme, *Newsline*, has broadcast a gripping programme incorporating the American footage. This consists of two parts. The first is video and audio recording of Col. Hayes in his Apache helicopter which show the targets and provide the exchanges between the pilot and his ground controllers. Then follows a long interview with Col. Hayes who has now left the US forces as he seeks partly to justify himself, partly to protest at what he considers his unfair victimization at the hands of the military authorities.

The footage is extraordinary but even more revealing are the verbal exchanges which show the pressure to destroy targets that was placed on US pilots. The Apache helicopters had been sent to look for Iraqi armour at a specific area. They find nothing and turning east they come across two armoured personnel carriers which seem not to be connected to the main US forces. The attack took place shortly after midnight so the question of a visual search for allied identifications is not relevant. All that Col. Hayes saw (and the viewers see) was a blurred shape on his cockpit video screen. Here he makes a crucial mistake. He misreads the grid number on the screen and reads back to his ground controller the original reference number for the area he had first been sent to.

Assuming that the Apache is over the enemy-held area, the ground controller shouts at Hayes, "Take 'em out, take 'em out." Hayes, the pilot is hesitant. Recalling perhaps General Horner's injunction, 'If in doubt, don't drop' (i.e. fire a missile), Lt. Col. Hayes seeks to fire his less-lethal cannon at the vehicles. The cannon jams. All the time, there is a persistent nag from the ground controller, "Take 'em out, take 'em out", sounding for all the world as if he was talking about removing a pair of steers from a herd for branding.

"Boy, I'm going to tell you, it's hard to pull this trigger" Hayes says hesitantly, still unsure about the vehicles' identity. But from the ground comes the incessant, war-happy incantation to "Take 'em out." Hayes unleashes his Hellfire missile which is seen arcing down to the vehicle which exploded. He fires a second one which "takes out" the second vehicle.

But now, the ground controller, previously so enthusiastic to kill, realises his mistake and tells Hayes that the vehicles were American Bradleys. "I was afraid of that, I was really afraid of that. I just killed a bunch of people," the US pilot announces sadly.

The Apache is the US military's most sophisticated, high-tech, and most expensive attack helicopter. Its crews are highly trained. But in this case, all the technology in the world cannot prevent a pilot from reading off an incorrect grid reference and all the training in the world cannot hold back soldiers who are desperate for a kill and make them think twice and three times to ensure that they are engaging the enemy.

In his lengthy exculpatory interview with American television, Hayes said: "I was out there fighting like everybody else and I had a terrible war accident. Where are all the other people who shot the friendly fire accidents?"

Hayes is convinced that he was dismissed from the US Army because his name somehow leaked out immediately and the US military authorities wanted to get rid of a potential media embarrassment. But officially, Hayes was relieved of his command four days after the incident because as a senior officer he should have been directing the battle not in the front line fighting and shooting at targets.

Here we are getting perhaps close to one reason which may explain what happened when the Fusiliers were killed. To gain combat experience and in the heat of battle fire a weapon that destroys the enemy is what is known in the US military as "career-enhancing." To have been in combat is to "punch your ticket" and open the way to further promotion. General Schwarzkopf was honest about the need to have combat experience in an interview he gave to an American writer in the 1970s: "I would be foolish if I said I was unaware that commanding a battalion in Vietnam would help my career. Of course it would!"

Firing and being fired back by people who want to kill you is the most effective training for a soldier which explains why the British Army has willingly undertaken all sorts of missions from the policing of the back streets of Derry in Ireland to working in what is almost a mercenary role for various Arab sheikdoms in order to keep in trim its soldiering skills under conditions which can never be reproduced on exercises.

The Americans psyched up their pilots by nightly briefings on Iraqi atrocities in Kuwait. Apache pilots were said to enjoy "coming in dry, with no bullets but big smiles." In the slaughter on the last day of the war, when for seven hours American aircraft pounded the Mutla Ridge over which the highway to Basra runs, hundreds — some estimates say scores of thousands — of soldiers and civilians fleeing from Kuwait City were killed. Any US aircraft that could fly was up in the sky. Planes were stacked as they are when there are too many trying to land at Heathrow and three US airborne air traffic controllers guided a plane in every 90 seconds so that the pilot could take part in the "turkey shoot" and say that he had fired his weapons and destroyed a target in the Gulf War.

Combining both the evidence from Col. Hayes and the lusting desire to kill expressed in the Basra Road carnage we can begin to decipher what happened to Warriors 22 and 23 in the Fusiliers. There are two pilots who have had a long, unsatisfactory mission. They have been unable to fire their Maverick missiles. They have tried to machine-gun a sitting target but the strafing run was a fiasco. Their exchanges with the DALO had been perfunctory. There had been no reading back of grid references, no double checking of where they were. Their patience and fuel were low. Much longer and they would have to go back home, landing with the humiliation of being teased about coming in with the missiles unfired. They believe that below them is ground peopled only with Iraqis and then suddenly, in the clear desert air, there is a perfect target. A group of vehicles stopped dead and arranged in a higgledy-piggledy fashion rather like the lorries and other Iraqi vehicles they had seen. The target was not moving forward purposely to the front in a warlike column with its flags flying. On the contrary, the vehicles in the target area were all over the place doing nothing very much at all.

The war was going very well. American troops had arrived at the outskirts of Basra. Any moment now and it might be over. Thousands of US pilots have spent twenty or more years in the US air force without ever firing a weapon in combat, let alone killing the enemy. Was this their last chance, if not exactly for glory, to taste the real thing? What was the rank of the lead A-10 pilot? Was he like Col. Hayes, a senior officer, who was keen to do some fighting, to fire the guns and missiles himself not sit directing others to war? There was no time for second thoughts, no time to inspect closely the target. Hell, they knew where they where, they had just shot up some Iraqi lorries, the F-16 pilot had described the area, the DALO had said there were no friendlies. To delay, to check further would mean missing the target as their fuel — 2 hours and 15 minutes since they had last refuelled — was getting very low. Better to blast from high in the sky before the target on the ground could even hear or see them.

The decision was taken, the button was pressed, the Mavericks sped down to destroy; the technology would actually do the work of delivering death, but, at last, the fighters could feel they had fought.

This reconstruction of what happened is guesswork. To enter into the psychology of the two A-10 pilots is a matter for experts and, it must be stressed, we have no evidence from the two men themselves nor from their comrades and colleagues with whom they must have discussed the event.

Even, to repeat, if we assume the DALO gave unclear or falsely-interpreted instructions, it is impossible to believe the pilots' story, carefully elaborated four months after the event, and with each pilot telling the identical tale, that they could have flown low and failed through the binoculars to see one of the 120 odd Vs or 70 fluorescent panels on the 37 vehicles in C Company or the dozens of other vehicles of the 3rd Battalion on the flat desert plain.

Whether or not Fusiliers saw or did not see the A-10 planes — even though the pilots claim to have made two passes over the ground — is not relevant. Whether from 8,000 feet or far lower, what happened was a quick see-and-shoot, hit-and-run attack.

Some fault can arguably lie with the DALO if he did not, as he claimed, provide accurate grid references to which the A-10s should have flown, but nothing excuses the American pilots' decision to attack the Warriors.

"If in doubt, don't drop," General Horner says the US pilots were told. Little was certain and there was plenty to doubt over grid reference 418518 in the southern Iraq desert on Tuesday afternoon, 26 February 1991: it did not stop someone pressing a trigger and stupidly, negligently, needlessly ending nine young lives.

CHAPTER 8

The US Cover-Up

By the time the A-10 pilots landed back in their base in Saudi Arabia they would have known they had been responsible for a disaster. Under section 15-6 of the US Uniform Code of Military Justice any death of a serviceman caused by other soldiers has to be investigated thoroughly. It is up to the investigating officers to decide whether further investigation should be undertaken, a reprimand issued, or that the case warrants court martial. The term court martial sounds sinister with guilt and punishment prejudged but it is no more or less than a trial in which the accused is presumed innocent and has the benefit of a defending attorney to ensure that the rules of evidence and court procedure are followed.

The courts martial that often get attention in the British press are when a naval officer crashes his ship into another boat or a jetty, or an aircraft pilot ejects when there does not appear to be a reason for doing so. Careers are ruined for doing damage to military property even if no person is hurt. In this case, nine people were killed but far from having a court martial the US Air Force appears to have not even carried out a full investigation. Because the dead were British, it has been the British authorities who have undertaken the most thorough investigation, but the armed services responsible for those killing the Fusiliers have sought to sweep the tragedy under the carpet.

But this rule is not applied to US friendly fire casualties. Americans killed 35 of their own military personnel in the Gulf War. 21 out of 89 US Army casualties were from friendly fire. In each case, a lieutenant colonel or higher ranking officer investigated the death. Technically, this was not necessary as provisions such as the 15-6 investigation which is mandatory in peacetime incidents is suspended when at war. According to Captain Tom Barth, aide to Lieutenant General Horner, commander of the US Air Force in the Gulf, the A-10 pilots were not subject to any investigation when they landed or in the immediate aftermath when it was realised what they had done.

Speaking to me from the Florida, USA, Central Command headquarters (the US Central Command, although based in Florida, is the US armed forces group responsible for covering the Middle East. General Schwarzkopf headed Central Command before his retirement when General Horner took over), Captain Barth said there had been some discussion "to review safety aspects of the incident" but he assured me that there had been no investigation and there existed no documents based on the immediate de-briefing of the two A-10 pilots.

If this is true, again, it is incredible. Two pilots have returned from a mission in which their only achievement was that they killed nine British soldiers and no one in the US Air Force asks any serious questions of them? Even more incredible is the implication that since the scale of the tragedy was known to Whitehall within 24 hours of it happening, no British minister pressed the Pentagon to provide an immediate, full report on what happened.

"Believe me, we have sent the British Ministry of Defence, everything we have got, sir. I repeat, to my knowledge there is no secret document that is being withheld from our side," Captain Barth insisted to me. He refused to confirm whether the video recordings which are normally automatically taped whenever a military aircraft fires guns or missiles were still in existence or if they had been sent to London in response to any request from the Ministry of Defence.

The only fully released account of a friendly fire incident — the one in which the Apache helicopter piloted by Lt. Col. Hayes destroyed the US armoured personnel carriers — shows that video and audio recordings were kept of what the pilots and ground controllers were saying to each other and what the aircraft's weapon system was seeing. As every television viewer saw in the Gulf War, the US military had video recordings showing the passage and arrival on target of many different weapons. It is normal air traffic control procedure to record exchanges so that if any allegation of error is made there is an immediate check on what was said.

Again, it is hard to accept that neither the Americans nor the British have no recording whatsoever of the exchanges that took place in the thirty minutes between the A-10s arriving in the general vicinity of the area and the unleashing of their missiles.

In treating their own citizens, the American authorities have also sought to cover up or delay telling the truth about what happened to the 35 American military personnel who died in friendly fire incident in the war.

The *Washington Post* reporter, Bart Gellman, investigated many of these cases and in an exposé published in the paper in November 1991 he revealed "a pattern of delay or denial affecting nearly every family that lost a serviceman to friendly fire in the Persian Gulf War". The US Army's treatment of its friendly fire cases is different from the British cover-up because in the case of the Americans the US military either did not reveal that casualties were from friendly fire and claimed instead that the soldiers had died from Iraqi attacks. Casualty reports were altered by higher echelons in the military. Reports that had typed on them "hit by friendly fire" had the words crudely crossed out to be replaced by a handwritten "vehicle hit by enemy fire."

Relatives were told that wounded soldiers died after receiving prompt medical care or the last sacraments in the case of a soldier of Catholic faith. These letters, taken from a US Army manual for form letters, were untrue as the soldiers concerned had died trapped in their vehicles. In some cases, the discovery that soldiers in armoured personnel carriers had been killed by friendly fire only came about when the wrecks were surveyed with a geiger counter. The examination showed that the shells which destroyed the vehicles were depleted uranium shells, a new deadly armour piercing round used by allied tanks.

Comrades of the US soldiers killed by friendly fire were told to keep quiet. The mother of one dead US soldier was given the truth by one of his comrades but then he "was told to shut his mouth," she said. The mother told the *Washington Post*, "One of his higher-ups said if he opened his mouth he could be court-martialled. He would not say who told him that. He was afraid to." (Similar threats were made to Fusilier Howard Finnan who was interviewed by the *Independent* about what happened when his Warrior was hit by an American rocket. He was told that if he talked again to the press he could face sanctions from the Army.)

In fact, it took until August 1991, before all 35 families of the US soldiers killed by friendly fire were officially informed of the cause of death of their children. "I feel betrayed," said one mother. The parents of a US Army sergeant were first told he had been killed "in an enemy firefight" but the father persisted until he was told that his son had been killed by a mini-bomb dropped by the Americans. "Not knowing, it leaves you hanging in the air like a rag in the wind," said the father expressing a sentiment identical to that of the Thompsons, the Atkinsons, the Gillespies and the other families of the dead Fusiliers in England.

So although the parents have been assured that the US authorities have provided all the information they have to the British Government, the evidence of how the Americans sought to cover up aspects of their own friendly fire deaths points to the almost certain probability that the US may be telling less than the whole truth.

The responsibility thus falls back on the British Government to press much harder for details of what happened from the US point of view and, in particular, to insist that the A-10 pilots are comprehensively interviewed (even with their anonymity being respected) by military and forensic experts so that a complete account of what happened in the southern Iraqi desert at 3 p.m. on Tuesday 26 February can be established.

CHAPTER 9

Peace of Mind

There is a parallel in the United States to the Thompsons' struggle in England. On 18 February 1970 an American soldier, Michael Mullen, was killed on a hill in Vietnam by US artillery fire. One of the best of the Vietnam war books, *Friendly Fire*, by C.D.B. Bryan, published in 1976, described the lengthy struggle of Mullen's parents to find out how their son had died against all the efforts by the Pentagon to cover up the details.

Like Lee Thompson, Michael Mullen was in a C Company when his life ended because of a mistake by his own side. His parents received standard condolence letters but became convinced that the full truth of how and why their boy had died was being withheld from them. As they tried to penetrate the Pentagon smokescreen they got some help from an unusual quarter.

The Mullens were able to meet with their son's commanding officer, an ambitious young officer with a babyish face and blonde hair. The officer, who had been wounded while saving the life of a solider in a mine-field, willingly agreed to meet with the Mullens while he was recuperating in a hospital in Washington. Later he met with the writer, Bryan, and discussed in detail not only the individual case of Michael Mullen's death by friendly fire but the wider implications of an army's duty to the relatives of its soldiers and the role of an army in a democratic society.

The officer's name was Lt. Col. H. Norman Schwarzkopf and with his help the Mullens came to find some peace of mind as they finally got to the bottom of why their boy was killed.

Twenty years later, General Schwarzkopf has said nothing about the Thompsons's search for the truth beyond a general expression of regret for the loss of the nine soldiers in the friendly fire incident. His deputy in the Gulf War, Lt. Gen. Horner, told the BBC's Brown and Shukman that those campaigning for the truth were "picking at a scab."

It is an unfortunate metaphor, insulting to the parents and, even if, as the General insists, he was talking about the journalists who have written on friendly fire deaths, it is condescending about reporters seeking to uncover an important public truth.

Because there is more, far more to this story than the grief of the Thompsons and their feeling that they have been pushed around by the powers that be, neither told the complete truth nor given all the information in the Government's possession. 40 per cent of the British servicemen killed in action in the Gulf war were killed as a result of friendly fire incidents. The new technology of warfare cannot easily distinguish between friend and foe. The unsettled world order we are now entering may require more deployment and action by British troops. We may hope that politicians have the vision to develop mechanisms to avert invasions or what are seen as unacceptable threats to national, regional, or global security, but Britain's existing policy of arming and supporting dictatorships in different corners of the world leaves little hope that peace and human rights will ever be given priority sufficient to lessen the impulses that lead to war. In a similar vein, writing about the United States, the New York professor, Edward Said, declared: "The main task for Americans is to figure out how this country's staggering power can be harnessed for communal coexistence with other socities, rather than for violence against them."

Alternatively, here in Britain, we may have the modesty and maturity to decide that Britain's day as a world policeman, or special constable tagging along behind the United States, is over. "Unhappy the land without heroes," says a character in a Brecht play. "Unhappy the land that has need of heroes," comes the reply. Britain has its Col. 'H' Jones VC from the Falklands and the battered faces of Tornado pilots from the Gulf or, in our recent past, one politician who saw herself as a world colossus, a new Boadicea. But is it not conceivable that our country might be much better off, our people might die peacefully in their beds, and our politicians might rule better by consensus, if we slowly let our militarism become part of our history instead of the object of panting desire whenever a disagreeable event takes place somewhere in the world?

Our future must lie in training all our people to produce socially-useful, profitable commodities and services we and the world need — either as products for sale or as public goods paid for by society. Curiously enough we do have an impressive public service, a nationalized institution under strict government

UNITED STATES CENTRAL COMMAND
OFFICE OF THE DEPUTY COMMANDER IN CHIEF AND CHIEF OF STAFF
MACDILL AIR FORCE BASE, FLORIDA 33608-7001

Air Marshal Sir John Kemball KCB CBE BA RAF
Headquarters Strike Command
Royal Air Force
High Wycombe
Buckinghamshire
United Kingdom

Dear Air Marshall Kemball,

Although we have spoken on the telephone about the
circumstances surrounding the unfortunate loss of lives and
injuries in a fratricide incident involving our forces, I wanted
to take this opportunity to respond more formally to your
inquiry. It appears to be virtually impossible to fully
ascertain exactly what happened on 26 February 1991 that caused
our A-10 aircraft to engage your Warrior Infantry Fighting
Vehicles. We have done our best to gather information from the
people involved and to use their recollections along with the
information you provided to determine the causal factors which
led to this incident. I have limited my comments to two specific
factors that we believe were the critical elements which lead to
the engagement.

The most significant factor which caused this incident was a
conflict in positional data. Quite simply, the incident pilots
thought they had been cleared to attack in the area in which they
were operating. We reviewed the statements in your letter and
the incident pilots original statements, and obtained additional
statements from the pilots to determine what attack position was
passed to the A-10 flight. There are discrepancies in the
statements from the DALO ███████████ and the A-10 pilots ███████████
as to what attack position was passed from the air controller to
the aircraft. Your letter states an assistant DALO briefed the
pilots to attack armour on ███████████ at grid reference point ██████.
The pilots state the DALO passed grid reference ███████████ (█████
for the target and that they had never heard the word ██████
until the incident investigation. However, the pilots did
receive a brief from the flight of F-16 aircraft ███████ which
preceded them, and verified in their own minds that they were in
the right area by visually sighting a departing F-16 and by
correlating reference points passed during their turnover
briefing. The pilots state that the DALO informed them "there
are no friendlies within 10 km" and cleared them for delivery of
weapons. The FSCL was well north of the operation area and
accordingly, the aircraft were operating under close air support
procedures. After being cleared to attack, the aircraft were

I am hopeful that the statements provided by the two pilots meet your needs and that we can close this unfortunate incident.

SIGNED ON ORIGINAL

R. B. Johnston
Major General, U.S. Marine Corps
Deputy Commander in Chief
   and Chief of Staff

control, and which has shown a level of professionalism, delivery, training and leadership rarely seen in the private sector. It is called the British Army, but it is a poor society that can produce a superbly-professional army but not find jobs for the homeless in its streets or create wealth to keep its hospitals open.

The Army will continue to have a role and may, alas, be again called upon to fight. If so, and particularly if it is to fight alongside the Americans, then it would be better if far fewer than four out of ten casualties were the result of friendly fire. British soldiers deserve a better future than to be target practice for American pilots.

That is the wider meaning of the Thompsons' struggle for the truth and the scandal of the continuing Government cover-up. Nothing can bring back their son, Lee, but the future Fusiliers of the British Army have a right to know that if they go into war jammed together in the back of their Warriors they have a better than two in five chance, if killed or wounded, of the death or injury being the responsibility not of the enemy but of their own side.

The Prime Minister, John Major, insists there has been no cover-up, no withholding of information. This is not true. In the words of his Conservative Party chairman, Chris Patten, Mr Major has told a "porky." The Americans themselves sent to the parents, via the British embassy, copies of letters which the US military had sent to senior British officers. The copies had vital information of key importance to the parents' campaign for the truth blacked out.

But the original letters lie in the files of the British Government, each word as easy to read today as when the envelopes were opened. In addition, there are the minutes of the Board of Inquiry, the interviews and reports of the investigating officers. There are various recordings of exchanges between the participants in the tragedy which at least one person I have spoken to claims to have heard. All these are suppressed by the Government despite repeated requests by the parents that they be told the full truth. That is the information that has been covered up, those are the details the Government has withheld and if Mr Major cannot understand that he is either a fool or a fibber.

Alternatively he is what Conor Cruise O'Brien, writing of someone else, called "a man of excellent intentions, boundless faith and limited political intelligence. It is not a reassuring combination." Mr Major puts a traditional interest of probably a majority of conservative British political figures — an unquestioning fidelity to America — before the interests of the citizens he represents and leads. However Mr Major is guilty of more than a cover-up. He has not protested, publicly if need be, to the White House. Mr Major has not demanded from his 'friend' President Bush that the full facts as known to the Americans, particularly their recordings and if necessary an in-depth questioning of the A-10 pilots plus all data from their mission, be made available.

When the French sent army experts to damage the Greenpeace organization's efforts to stop French nuclear testing in the Pacific, a French officer went too far and killed a photographer on the Greenpeace boat, "Rainbow Warrior", as it was moored in Auckland, New Zealand. In the end, after considerable pressure from the New Zealand government, the French government apologized. The French Prime Minister, Michel Rocard, travelled to New Zealand and said "Sorry." The parents of the nine soldiers killed by the American pilots in the Gulf are still waiting for the pilots' commander-in-chief, President George Bush, to say "Yes, we were responsible and, on behalf of the United States, I am sorry."

"The struggle of man against power is the struggle against forgetting," writes the Czech novelist, Milan Kundera. The Government hopes that time will wash away the hurt caused by the loss of Lee Thompson. Let us hope it will because to live permanently in grief is no life. But the best help the Government can give to the Thompsons to come to terms with what happened is to tell them what happened.

The psychologist, Elizabeth Kuhler-Ross, an expert on grief and recovery, has said:

> Honesty is always the best policy, otherwise they go through the shock and the anger and anguish and then they begin to recuperate and then they go through it all ten times worse. It helps them to know the truth. It will be shocking at first, but it's much more shocking if they discover it later on.

What did happen in that barren part of the world on 26 February 1991? Short of talking with the two pilots, we cannot finally say. Mick and Barbara Thompson are convinced that the A-10 pilots were "Rambos who had to get a notch on their gun", but this is to enter into the mentality and motives of the pilots not to deal in the evidence available. Lee is dead; his body lies buried in Coventry where fresh flowers are placed on it every weekend; his memory is still warm in the hearts of his parents, brothers and sister, and friends. His death was that of a soldier in action. As he breathed his last, he was with his comrades-in-arms taking part in a war that he believed to be just. His memory is not impugned by asking that those he left behind should be trusted with the whole truth.

Half a century ago when the United States went to war against evil it had more intelligent leaders. They ensured that the sacrifice made by allied troops did not leave in place the dictators who had invaded their neighbours or who had ruled with torture and brutality over their own people. The US Secretary of War in World War Two was a wise old politician called Henry Stimson. At the end of his career he remarked: "After many years in public life I have learnt that the only way to make people trustworthy is to trust them."

Our Government is not prepared to trust the Thompsons, indeed our rulers in the broadest sense are profoundly reluctant to trust the people. "It is better to win without fighting than to win every battle," says a Japanese proverb. The Thompsons do not want to fight, do not require a victory. They simply want the truth about how and why their son, Lee, died. Is it too much to ask?

APPENDIX A

Letter from Ministry of Defence to Mick and Barbara Thompson together with summary of the Board of Inquiry's report

Secretary of State
Ministry of Defence
Whitehall
London SW1A 2HB

23 July 1991

Dear Mr Thompson,

The Secretary of State has asked me to send you a full account of the findings of the Board of Inquiry into the tragic incident in the Gulf conflict in which your son was killed on 26th January.

The Board of Inquiry has now reported and its findings have been considered. A full account of these (and the details of 3 other incidents in which British personnel were wounded by friendly fire) will be given in an Answer to Parliament at 1530 tomorrow afternoon.

I enclose a copy of the Answer for your information but the Secretary of State thought you might like to note some issues in particular.

First, the weather at the time of the incident was clear, although there had been an intense sandstorm earlier in the day; and C Company was stationary after earlier fighting. Unfortunately a number of early accounts, which reached the United Kingdom and were passed on in good faith, were mistaken on these points.

Secondly, the Board concluded that 3 Royal Regiment of Fusiliers was in no way to blame for the incident. All its vehicles were correctly displaying the inverted "V" and fluorescent panels. It is clear that the two Warriors were attacked by two USAF A-10 aircraft, which should have attacked Iraqi armour more than 20 kilometres to the east of C Company's position. The pilots said that they identified their target from a description given to them by aircraft who had previously attacked the correct target.

There is a conflict of evidence between the pilots of the aircraft and the British Assistant Divisional Air Liaison Officer (DALO) about whether the pilots were given the grid reference for the Iraqi target. The Board has recommended that procedures should be tightened up to ensure that the co-ordinates for a target are always given to and acknowledged by the aircraft pilot.

The Secretary of State wanted you to have the fullest account of this tragic accident. He very much regrets that, in spite of all our efforts, the Board could not resolve the conflict of evidence over why the aircraft were in the wrong place and why the two Warrior vehicles were misidentified. It is clear that all UK and USAF personnel were striving to achieve their individual tasks. Given the understandable pressure of events on all those involved, it is inevitable that, at some stage, difficulties may arise.

Yours sincerely,

(MISS J R BINSTEAD)

Private Secretary

Summary of the Board of Inquiry Prepared for Submission to Parliament

There were four incidents during the Gulf conflict in which British soldiers were killed or injured by friendly forces. Nine soldiers were killed and sixteen injured in these incidents. The Board of Inquiry into the incident when nine soldiers were killed and eleven injured in two Warrior vehicles belonging to the 3rd Battalion the Royal Regiment of Fusiliers Battle Group (3 RRF) has now reported. It has been the practice of successive Governments not to publish reports of this kind, but I wish to give as full an account as possible of the Board's findings.

On 26 February 1991, 3 RRF had fought their way through a number of enemy positions in southern Iraq. After a brief but intense sandstorm during the early part of the advance, the weather had improved to give clear skies and good visibility by about 1500 hours local time, when C Company 3 RRF, with some 37 Warrior and Engineer vehicles, was reorganising. The terrain in the area was flat and featureless apart from some Iraqi defensive positions and abandoned vehicles and equipment. During the reorganisation, Royal Engineers prepared to destroy nearby Iraqi artillery pieces. When the demolition charges were about to be blown, C Company Commander instructed his men to reenter their vehicles, close hatches and move away from the gun emplacements.

8 Platoon had been stationary and out of their vehicles for about 15 minutes before this order was given. As they started to comply, one Warrior, callsign 22, exploded. Another Warrior, callsign 23, immediately manoeuvred in front of callsign 22, and some crew members had just begun to move the casualties to the first aid post when callsign 23 also exploded. A-10 aircraft were seen in the area at the time of the explosions, but at first mines were suspected.

Earlier during the day, two successive flights of United States Air Force (USAF) aircraft were tasked by Headquarters 1st (British) Armoured Division to attack Iraqi armour at grid reference PT6857.

Subsequently, a further flight of two USAF A-10 aircraft reported for tasking to the British Assistant Divisional Air Liaison Officer (DALO). His intention was that these aircraft should attack the same target as the two previous flights but there is a conflict of evidence over whether a grid reference for the target was passed from the Assistant DALO to the A-10s. The target location was over 20KM to the east of C Company 3 RRF's position at 1500 hours.

The A-10 pilots identified what they thought was the target area from a physical description given them by a departing USAF F-16 of the previous flight, and shortly afterwards saw what they thought were about 50 Iraqi T54/55 tanks and support vehicles heading north. The pilots had been told that there were no friendly forces within 10 kilometres of their target, and these vehicles were closer than that to the point they had identified as their target. The lead aircraft made two passes, at 15,000 and 8,000 feet, to observe the vehicles with binoculars, but saw no friendly markings. Both aircraft then fired one infra-red Maverick missile from a height of about 9,000 feet, each destroying one of the vehicles, before reporting the engagement to the Assistant DALO and leaving the area.

The pilots' report of 50 Iraqi vehicles differed so dramatically from earlier descriptions of the target that the Assistant DALO asked them to confirm the location. The flight leader reported that the attack had taken place at grid reference PT 418518. The Assistant DALO immediately realised that this position was more than 20 kilometres from the intended target and corresponded with the location of 3 RRF. He then called up a reconnaissance flight over the area, which reported that fluorescent air recognition panels could be seen from 6,000 feet and the type of vehicles could be identified from 14,000 feet.

The Board of Inquiry found that 8 Platoon, C Company 3 RRF were on operations as ordered. The Board also found that the air planning procedures allowing a distance of more than 15 kilometres between the target for any air attack and friendly forces had been followed and should have been sufficient to ensure the successful and safe conduct of operations. The Board further concluded that air control at Corps and Divisional level which provided tasking information to the A-10s was in accordance with established procedures.

The Board found that 8 Platoon's vehicles were displaying correct inverted V recognition symbols and fluorescent panels. The Board noted that some of the panels could have been partially obscured by open hatches or equipment, and that while a reconnaissance flight observed the panels at 6,000 feet, this was below the operating height of the A-10s. The Board could not make any finding as to whether the pilots should have seen the identification panels at their operating height.

The Board concluded that no blame or responsibility for the incident could be attributed to 3 RRF.

The Board noted that there was a conflict of evidence between the statements of the witnesses from Headquarters 1st (British) Armoured

Division and those of the A-10 pilots. The Assistant DALO stated that he passed the target grid reference but the A-10 pilots deny receiving this. There was no evidence to suggest that the two previous missions had attacked anything but the correct targets. On the evidence presented, the Board found that no blame or responsibility should be attached to the Assistant DALO.

The pilots stated that, notwithstanding the absence of a grid reference, they attacked on the basis of information passed to them by the previous flight and of their positive identification of the targets as enemy vehicles. The Board noted that a USAF reconnaissance flight shortly after the Warriors were attacked was able to identify the types of vehicles from 14,000 feet. On the basis of the evidence before it, the Board was unable to establish why the attacked Warrior vehicles were misidentified by the A-10 pilots as enemy T54/55 tanks, particularly in view of their previous identification runs at 8,000 and 15,000 feet. In forwarding the Board's findings, the Joint Commander has drawn attention to the way in which aspect, weather and light conditions can critically affect a pilot's ability to identify the detail of objects on the ground.

The Board did not establish whether the USAF personnel involved were at fault. It was clearly established that the USAF A-10s delivered the missiles, but the Board could not establish precisely why they attacked the wrong target.

The Board remarked that it was clear that all UK and USAF personnel involved were striving to achieve their individual tasks to the best of their abilities in a fast-moving battle. The Board thought it inevitable that, at some stage, difficulties may arise when individuals are under such pressure. On 26 February 1991 difficulties arose in relation to the location and identification of the target, and the Board concluded that only the clearest of standard operating procedures and sophisticated identification systems will help to prevent such tragedies in the future.

The Board recommended that a study be initiated to identify a suitable air recognition system for future use, confirmed the importance of standard operating procedures for the control of aircraft in offensive air support operations and recommended that they must always include instructions that a grid reference or a latitude and longitude is specifically included in mission briefs and that this is always acknowledged by pilots.

The Government (and the United States Administration) wish to express their deepest sympathy and condolences to the relatives of those who died in this tragic incident.

During the conflict there were a further three incidents involving friendly fire in which British Servicemen were injured.

The first of these occurred shortly after 1100 local time on 26 February. An officer attached to 1 Staffords received shrapnel wounds when a Warrior vehicle was attacked by a Challenger tank of the Scots Dragoon Guards. Personnel from 1 Staffords were guarding prisoners of war when a Challenger tank from the Scots Dragoon Guards began to engage nearby Iraqi armoured vehicles, which later turned out to be abandoned. The tank mistakenly fired on the vehicles of 1 Staffords, hitting the Warrior, before moving off. Visibility at the time was reduced by a dust storm to about 400 metres. All the Staffords' vehicles were marked with the inverted V Device and carried fluorescent orange panels. The four personnel in the Warrior were unharmed, but shrapnel injured an officer who had dismounted from another vehicle. Once the mistake was realised, the Scots Dragoon Guards returned to the scene and evacuated the officer to hospital.

Another incident occurred shortly before 1100 local time on 27 February. Two personnel from the Queen's Royal Irish Hussars (QRIH) were injured when their Scorpion armoured reconnaissance vehicles were fired on by US M1 Abrams tanks. Both Scorpions were carrying the black inverted V device and visibility was good. UK and US forces had their own areas of operations and the QRIH Reconnaissance Section was about 2 kilometres within its area. They had stopped to take the surrender of Iraqi troops, when one Scorpion was hit in the front by a round from a US M1 tank, firing from about 1500 metres to the North. The driver escaped without injury, but a soldier walking alongside received shrapnel wounds. The other Scorpion came under tank and machine gun fire, and the soldier manning the turret-mounted machine gun also received shrapnel wounds. When the US personnel realised their mistake they assisted with the treatment of the injured British soldiers and their evacuation to hospital.

The third incident also occurred on 27 February. At about 1445 local time, two soldiers from 10 Air Defence Battery, Royal Artillery received burns when two Spartan armoured vehicles from which they had dismounted were engaged by Challenger tanks from 14/20 Hussars with thermal sights beyond the range of unaided visibility (about 1500 metres). In these conditions, it was not possible to identify the inverted V device carried by the vehicles. The rearmost vehicle was hit and burst into flames. The other vehicle was also damaged in the ensuing fire. The Spartan destroyed was empty and was being towed after breaking down. The Spartans had become detached from a convoy of 7th Armoured Brigade vehicles which had been delayed in getting clear of the area because of the difficult terrain.

Letter from Prime Minister John Major to Mick and Barbara Thompson

The Prime Minister
10 Downing Street
London SW1A 2AA

13 November, 1991

Dear Mr and Mrs Thompson,

Thank you for your letter of 2 October. I am sorry that I have not replied before now, but I wanted to go into all the points you raised.

Please do not think we are unsympathetic or indifferent to your loss. I understand the grief and shock that Lee's death must have brought to you, and I was very moved by the obituary to Lee in *The Fusilier*. My heart goes out to you.

I know that Tom King too understands your suffering, and was pleased to have been able personally to express his condolences when he met you at the City of London Welcome Home Parade in June.

I know that waiting for the outcome of the Board of Inquiry into the incident only added to your heartache. But it was very important for the Board to pursue all lines of investigation into the tragedy so that the clearest possible account could be established. This was a task that inevitably took a considerable time to complete. Mr Hamilton made the statement to Parliament as soon after the Board had submitted its report to the Ministry of Defence as possible. I can assure you that it was a pure coincidence that this was only just before the Summer Recess.

I believe that you have now received a letter from our Ambassador in Washington covering one from the US Government, which follows up President Bush's undertaking to look into the matter. Like us, the Americans wanted to make sure that there was no information that had been overlooked and that everything had been made available to the Board of Inquiry. Again, this took time, but the letter you have received confirms that the Americans have no additional information.

You asked a number of questions on the detail of the report of the incident, which I shall do my best to answer. I should make it clear, however, that Mr Hamilton's statement gave all the main facts presented to the Board of Inquiry. There is no question of anyone concealing information or covering anything up. We have been at pains to give you the clearest picture possible. I do appreciate that your grief might have been lessened if the Board had been able to allocate responsibility for the accident, but the information available simply does not enable this to be done.

I am aware of the additional distress that has been caused by apparently conflicting reports on the incident. The initial accounts given by members of the Regiment and others were given in good faith, based on information they had received from the Gulf. I very much regret that they later proved to be inaccurate and incomplete. It was to establish exactly what happened that the Board of Inquiry was convened.

Turning to your detailed questions, I confirm that the Warriors were fired on by the pilots of *two* A-10 aircraft: the statements of the pilots which have been sent to you by the US Government make this clear, though it may well not have been obvious to those on the ground at the time.

Tom King has assured me that he meant no discourtesy by not personally signing the letters that accompanied the report. He has taken a very close interest in this case and approved the text1 of the letter himself. Unfortunately, other commitments meant that he was unavailable to sign the letter when it was ready and he authorised his Private Secretary to sign it on his behalf.

I am very sorry that the letter contained the wrong date. There is no excuse for this — it was simply an error, for which I apologise unreservedly. As soon as Miss Binstead realised her mistake, she tried to telephone all the families to apologise in person, but I understand that most had already left for Germany. She therefore arranged for a written apology to be passed to each of you on arrival.

On the conflict of evidence, it is not a question of whether or not the A-10s were in the wrong place. It is a fact that they were. What the Board was unable to resolve was why they were in the wrong place: there is an unresolved conflict of evidence as to whether the grid reference pinpointing the current target was passed to the pilots. It was the practice in the case of deep close air support missions in the Gulf for a target grid reference to be passed to the pilots, who would also receive information about the target area from any preceding flight. In this case, the Assistant DALO stated that he passed the grid reference to the pilots: the pilots stated that they did not receive it. The pilots did, however, receive detailed topographical information from a pilot who had left the target area only shortly before. On the basis of this information, the pilots believed (wrongly) that they had correctly identified the target area. Since they had been briefed that there were no friendly forces within 10 kilometres of the target area, they further believed that they had positively identified enemy targets on the ground. In these circumstances, they would have seen no need to make further contact with the Assistant DALO before attacking.

There is no explanation why the A-10 pilots misidentified the Warriors as T54/T55 tanks and did not see the identification panels that they carried. The Board of Inquiry could not reach a conclusion on this, but it is perhaps worth noting that in forwarding the Board's report, the Joint Commander made the point that he knew from personal experience that the degree of detail of ground objects visible from the air can critically depend on the line of sight in relation to the sun.

You asked why the A-10s had attacked when there was no threat to them from ground forces. At the time, 1st (British) Armoured Division was in the middle of its advance through Southern Iraq. United States aircraft were providing deep close air support to all coalition ground forces, and in this case, were being tasked by the Divisional Headquarters to attack Iraqi armour to assist 4th Brigade to achieve the objectives it had been set. Thus, while the Royal Regiment of Fusiliers were actually at rest when the Warriors attacked, the battle was still being joined by British ground forces generally, and the Iraqis remained a threat to them.

On the question of drug-testing, I do not believe that anyone involved would have seen the need. The pilots were actively engaged on operational missions and made a most tragic error. There has never been any suggestion that this was due to any physical cause.

The statement made by Mr Hamilton to the House of Commons included the other friendly fire incidents because this was a formal report to Parliament on all such cases. I can assure you that there was no intention that the mention of the other incidents should distract attention from the account of the one in which your son was killed.

I hope that this letter will bring you some peace of mind and help you to come to terms with your loss. Once again, please accept my deepest sympathies.

Yours Sincerely,

John Major

APPENDIX C

Letter from US Assistant Secretary for Defense Carl Ford to British Ambassador in Washington

The Assistant Secretary of Defense
Washington, D.C. 20301-2400

His Excellency Sir Robin Renwick
Embassy of the United Kingdom of Great Britain and
Northern Ireland
3100 Massachusetts Avenue, N.W.
Washington, D.C. 20008

4 November 1991

Dear Mr Ambassador:

At the request of President Bush, the Department of Defense has re-examined all information possessed by the US Government concerning the "friendly fire" incident of February 26, 1991, in which nine British soldiers were killed and 11 wounded by Maverick missiles fired from United States Air Force A-10 aircraft during Operation Desert Storm.

Since the casualties were British subjects, the investigation of this incident was carried out by Her Majesty's government. The US government fully cooperated with the British Board of Inquiry by providing all information in our possession to the Board. Our primary concern in answering the President's request was to determine if any additional information exists which was not provided to the Board during the investigation. We have spoken with the air force component of the United States Central Command in addition to offices in the Pentagon which could conceivably have conducted a separate inquiry. Our search has turned up no new evidence, and we are convinced that no information has been withheld from Her Majesty's Government.

Because we did not conduct a separate investigation, we can only relate the circumstances of what happened from the perspective of the American A-10 pilots. Their mission was to locate and destroy fixed or moving enemy targets within an assigned target area. The A-10 pilots stated that no target coordinates were passed to them, although they were told by the British Assistant Divisional Air Liaison Officer (DALO) that friendly forces were not within 10 kilometers of the target area.

Additionally, an F-16 pilot from a previous attack passed a detailed verbal description of the target area to the A-10 pilots. The A-10 pilots identified a hard-surfaced road intersection and two burning hulks that matched this description. After making strafing passes on a supply vehicle, the A-10 flight leader saw a column of vehicles approximately one mile south of the vehicle they were strafing. The pilots made two passes over the convoy of vehicles looking for visual identification markings (orange panels) without seeing any friendly markings. In view of the lack of observable friendly markings, the pilots assessed that they were enemy vehicles and each pilot fired a Maverick missile. As they departed, the pilots passed a report to the British Assistant DALO, who asked for and received the target coordinates of the vehicles attacked.

The British Assistant DALO stated in his evidence that he had passed the target grid reference to the A-10 pilots; the A-10 pilots state that they never received this transmission, which had they received, they would have acknowledged. Under the circumstances, both statements are plausible.

In our re-examination of this incident, the A-10 pilots were asked and they agreed to release declassified versions of their statements. Copies of these statements, together with associated documents, are attached.

This incident is particularly upsetting since all parties involved were trying to protect the lives of their comrades. That the same technology responsible for the coalition's rapid victory with minimal loss of life should also take the lives of nine allied soldiers is tragic. Americans are no strangers to the type of suffering experienced by the families of the British victims; 32 Americans were killed and 72 wounded by friendly fire during the Gulf War. We are constantly searching for ways to eliminate friendly fire incidents, yet given the stressful, fast-paced environment of modern war, we cannot always prevent these accidents.

It is impossible to express fully the sense of loss we feel for fallen comrades in arms, and especially so in a case involving friendly fire. Please extend our deepest and most heartfelt sympathies to the families of the British soldiers. Our prayers are with them.

Sincerely,

Carl W. Ford, Jr.
Assistant Secretary of Defense
International Security Affairs